Changing Your Money Mindset

Changing Your Money Mindset

21 DAYS TO A MORE PRO$PEROU$ LIFE

Dr. Vicky Spring Love

Victory Jubilee Publishing
Southfield, Michigan

Unless otherwise indicated, all Scripture quotations are from the Holy Bible, New King James Version. Scripture quotations marked NIV are from the Holy Bible, New International Version, © 1973, 1978, 1984 by the International Bible Society. All rights reserved. All additions with italics or underline are the author's addition.

Please note that the name, satan, and related names are not capitalized. The author chooses not to acknowledge him, even to the point of violating grammatical rules.

Every effort has been made to present accurate information in this book. However, this book is not a substitute for professional financial or legal advice.

CHANGING YOUR MONEY MINDSET:
21 DAYS TO A MORE PROSPEROUS LIFE

Victory Jubilee Publishing
P. O. Box 3286
Southfield, Michigan 48037

Web site: www.ChangingYour MoneyMindset.com
E-mail: vickyspringlove@hotmail.com

ISBN: 0-9746883-1-2
Printed in the United States of America

Dedication

This book is dedicated to

Glen T. Love,

my husband, my best friend

and lifelong companion.

Thank you for your support

and for being my partner

in our quest to live

the prosperous life.

CONTENTS

INTRODUCTION

Our mindset about money can make all the difference in the world in how we respond to life's challenges and whether or not we fully participate in God's plan for prosperity for our lives. Some people have a poverty mindset, which becomes a stronghold on their lives. It affects the jobs they accept, the level of income they are comfortable with and the amount of prosperity their ultimately enjoy. A poverty mindset can come from many sources – your upbringing, the friends you associate with, a lack of vision and ignorance. But mostly it reflects a lack of faith in an all powerful, limitless God who has promised to do "exceedingly abundantly above all that we can ask or think." A poverty mindset can become a prison that limits your potential and effectiveness. But it can be broken out of through warfare with the Word.

The prosperity message has been misunderstood by the body of Christ because some ministers have misused the message of the Bible for their own personal gain and caused confusion in the church. This book seeks to bring balance to the teaching of prosperity based upon an examination of the scriptures. Prosperity covers every area of your life. It is not a get-rich-quick maneuver. Rather, it is living in God's abundance and blessings every day.

Prosperity begins in the mind because we become what we think about on a regular basis. This book lays out a process for transforming your mind by the Word of God. We tend to look at the results in our lives and want to make a change, however, change must happen first in your thought life before you will ever see a manifestation in other areas of your life.

Changing your money mindset requires an increase in your faith. There are different levels of faith that you can operate at in any given moment – no faith, little faith or great faith. The goal is to operate with great faith – a faith that acts on God's Word alone. We can increase our faith by meditating on the Word of God.

When you make the decision to develop a prosperous mindset, it requires that you learn to think in different ways. This book will show you not only how to think and what to think but provides you with a 21-day step-by-step plan to help you break the poverty mindset off your life forever and receive the abundant prosperity that God wants for your life.

Developing a prosperous mindset includes challenging yourself and your thinking patterns in every area. You will learn how to meditate on God's Word, what it means to honor God first, the importance of working hard, the need to stretch your faith by asking big requests of God, the role of discipline in creating your prosperity and much more. The Bible tells us in III John 1:2, "Beloved, I pray that you may prosper in all things and be in health, just as your soul prospers." God wants us to prosper in every area of life and this book will help you to do so.

Finally, all the tools and knowledge about prosperity is meaningless if you do not have a personal relationship with the Lord Jesus Christ. Eternal prosperity can be enjoyed once you have placed your trust in the savior of the world. He fills your heart with His peace, joy and precious Holy Spirit. Although you can put a monetary value on a lot of the benefits of prosperity, the value of eternal prosperity is priceless!

Chapter 1

The Prison of a Poverty Mindset

Have you ever known someone who is always struggling financially? Perhaps you have had more than your share of financial problems. For some people, financial struggle is their daily way of life. They have never known a time of financial peace, let alone financial prosperity.

Of course, I do recognize that there are regions of this world where there is a lack of natural resources causing people to live daily with limited material things.

However, I believe that no matter the outward conditions, the worst type of poverty is poverty thinking because it can destroy your faith and keep you trapped in limitation, lessened potential and dire circumstances.

So what is a poverty mindset? Darrow Miller, in his book Discipling Nations, gives insight into how a mindset of poverty affects people everywhere. "Except for catastrophic events such as war, drought, or flood, physical poverty doesn't 'just happen.' It is the logical result of the way people look at themselves and the world, the stories they tell to make sense of their world. Physical poverty is rooted in a mindset of poverty, a set of ideas held corporately that produce certain behaviors…Those with a poverty mind see the world through the glasses of poverty. They say or their actions say for them, 'I am poor, I will always be poor, and there is nothing I can do about it.'"

Poverty is not just a mindset but also a demonic spirit designed to limit your life, according to Rick Joyner in Overcoming the Spirit of Poverty. He writes, "When we think of poverty, we usually think of money or economics, but the spirit of poverty may or may not have anything to do with these. The spirit of poverty is a stronghold established for the purpose of keeping us from walking in the fullness of the victory gained for us at the cross, or the blessings of our inheritance in Christ. This can relate to everything from the quality of our marriages to the anointing we have for ministry, as well as any other resources that we need for what we have been called to do."

The first step out of poverty financially is to confront the poverty that is in your mind. In this chapter, we will look at examples of how a poverty mindset can affect your finances. You may see yourself in some of the examples given. My desire is to expose the lies that satan uses to keep people bound in lack and limitation.

Your Friends Can Limit You

When my husband and I were newly married, we had limited finances like most newlyweds. Although our finances were limited, our faith was strong. We walked in faith – tithing, giving and believing God for increase in our finances.

At the time, we were good friends with another couple, whom I'll call Mark and Linda (not their real names). Mark and my husband, Glen, would frequently talk about different issues of life, finances and family. The only problem with the relationship was that Mark had a poverty mindset. Perhaps it was our faith that irritated Mark because he would frequently say things like, "You guys are rich, we are not." Or "I know you guys tithe but my wife and I can't afford to tithe." Or "We don't have money like you do."

The problem with Mark's comments was that they simply were not true. Since he and Glen were good friends, they talked about everything including income. At that time, Mark and Linda actually made more money than we did! But our mindsets were miles apart. Because they had a poverty mindset, it kept them living in lack even to the point of refusing to tithe because they felt they couldn't afford it.

Because Glen and I had a different mindset, we never complained about money, even when we didn't have any! We trusted God and projected our faith in God regardless. We tithed and gave to the church, even when we felt we couldn't afford it. Why? Because we were truly trusting God to provide for our needs and we felt we had to honor God first to show our faith in Him.

As time went on, I became interested in real estate investing. I was watching late night TV and saw shows on how you could invest in real estate with no money down. I talked about my dreams of owning real estate and creating wealth through my investments. Only I was shot down by Linda big time. She boldly told me how the things I talked about "could never be done" and went on to tell me horror stories she heard from other landlords who had their rental properties destroyed by bad tenants.

I learned two things from my conversation with Linda. One, you have to be really careful who you share your dreams with. Some people cannot handle it when you have big ideas and plan to create wealth. The second thing I learned was that you cannot allow other people's negative experiences to deter you from what you dream of doing. If I had let her landlord horror stories affect me, I never would have purchased my first investment property.

It's been over 25 years since our conversations with Mark and Linda. As it turned out, I did invest in real estate and created so much profit that it not only increased our household income so I could become a stay-at-home mom but it also allowed me to build our college education fund that eventually helped pay for our children's college. And although I have had a few minor negative experiences with tenants, the vast majority of my tenants took excellent care of my properties and paid their rent on time. And when I sold my investment properties, I sold every one of them at a nice profit!

Over the years, we stopped hanging out with Mark and Linda. When you try to influence people positively and it continues to fall on deaf ear, you move on. Occasionally, Glen will run into Mark at some event. Mark is still struggling with income and not tithing. He'll still make comments like, "Well, you guys are rich."
Only now he's right.

Lack of Vision Can Hold You Back

A poverty mindset can manifest itself in a lack of vision for the future. You end up stuck in a financial rut, perhaps working a job that barely meets the financial needs of your household.

When you lack vision, it's hard for you to believe that God would give you an idea to take your household to prosperity. And if God does give you a big idea, you either will not follow up on it, or you will find a way to sabotage it. Your poverty mindset keeps you stuck where you are.

A friend of mine, whom I'll call William, was the head chef at a fancy restaurant in the suburbs. Although this restaurant had an awesome reputation and clients paid a huge bill to dine there, William was only paid a meager wage that was barely above the national median average income for households.

The Prison of a Poverty Mindset

William and his wife, Betty, had five children and Betty was a stay-at-home mom. William was an awesome chef and his meals always garnered rave reviews at the restaurant. At home, William liked to grill and created a marinade for his meat that was absolutely delicious. The marinade made the meat taste so good, you didn't need any barbeque sauce on it at all. In fact, if you wanted to put barbeque sauce on his meat, he was insulted!

One day William and Betty shared his grilled meat with a friend who absolutely loved it. This friend was a graphic artist who encouraged William that he should sell his marinade to retailers. He designed a label for the marinade and even had connections with a major national food chain to allow them to present their idea. The food chain loved it and wanted to test it locally, and then if it was successful, take it national.

But William and Betty were stuck in a poverty mindset. They began to argue about things like the design of the label, why his picture was on the label and not hers, how they would pay for producing the marinade for the national chain and on and on. Till finally, they wasted so much time that the window of opportunity closed and the national chain was no longer interested.

Since that time, William and Betty have continued to struggle financially, living on a meager income, taking out loans to pay for their children's college education and have almost lost their home to foreclosure on at least two occasions, looking to the church to bail them out of their financial woes.

Because they had a poverty mindset and did not have the vision to see a more financially prosperous future, they missed their opportunity and remained stuck in their poverty mindset.

God says in Habakkuk 2:2-4, "Write the vision and make it plain on tablets, that he may run who reads it. For the vision is yet for an appointed time; but at the end it will speak, and it will not lie. Though it tarries, wait for it; because it will surely come, it will not tarry. Behold the proud, his soul is not upright in him; but the just shall live by his faith."

I believe God has a vision for each person's life. That vision will allow you to live out your purpose and destiny utilizing the gifts and talents that God has blessed you with. In the process, it will produce the income you need to not only take care of the needs of your household but also it will create an overflow of wealth that you can use to help further the kingdom of God.

Fear will Keep You in a Poverty Mindset

The Bible tells us in Proverbs 8:12, "I wisdom dwell with prudence, and find out knowledge of witty inventions." I believe that God, through his wisdom, reveals new ideas and innovations to mankind. In fact, since God knows everything, He already knows what new inventions mankind is going to need to help solve our problems of the future. He is just looking for someone who will take the ideas that He gives and utilize them to create something new in the earth. God gives us ideas of things to invent.

I was teaching a class on Biblical Prosperity once and shared this verse with the class. One of my students, who I'll call Pam, raised her hand to make a comment. Pam told how the Lord had given her an idea of a gadget to invent that met a household need. She had shared the idea with a few trusted friends who thought it would be a great gadget to have.

However, Pam was plagued with self-doubt and fear. She didn't know how she would come up with the money to manufacture this gadget or the marketing connections to bring it to the marketplace. So she allowed fear to stop her. She didn't do anything with her idea. She never even tried to get the gadget manufactured and sold.

A few years later, Pam saw a similar gadget that served the same purpose advertised on television with the familiar slogan, "Only $19.95, call 1-800 … to get yours today!" She was both amazed to see it and mad at herself because she realized that the wealth from the sale of that gadget was supposed to be hers not someone else's. All those gadgets that end up on TV for $19.95 are making somebody rich, why not Pam?

Too often when God drops a "big" idea into our spirit, we allow fear and our own poverty mindset to stop us. We cannot "see" ourselves having a successful business. In our minds, we are not comfortable with that idea. The prosperity that comes to us will be the amount that we can comfortably handle; if it is beyond our comfort zone, we will mentally reject the idea.

It's important to understand that fear is a tool of the enemy designed to keep you in bondage. Fear has been defined as "false evidence appearing real". The thing that is limiting you is a deception from the enemy. Satan is a liar and the father of lies so he uses his power of deception to keep you in fear.

But God has given power to overcome that fear. In II Timothy 1:7 says, "For God has not given us a spirit of fear, but of power and of love and of a sound mind." We can allow fear to stop us or we can allow fear to cause us to develop courage. I love what Joyce Meyer says, "Do it afraid!" The fear is still there but you don't allow it to stop you.

Your Comfort Zone Can Destroy You

Too often we get stuck in our comfort zone, that place that we are comfortable in but that doesn't challenge us to move forward in our lives. Our comfort zone can be a certain level of income that we are comfortable in and can never get beyond. Or it can be a career that we have settled into that really is not fully utilizing the fullness of our talents and abilities.

When you are comfortable, your financial needs may be met but you don't have any excess left over. When you are comfortable, you have settled into a routine, a predetermined set of actions that you take on a regular basis to live your life. That's fine if what you have accomplished today is all that you ever want to accomplish.

However, if you want to move to another level, expand your income, start a business, launch your ministry, write your book, create prosperity or do anything new and different, it will require you to get outside of your comfort zone. You will have to try new activities, confront your fears and act in spite of them.

T. Harv Eker in his book, Secrets of the Millionaire Mind, states, "By expanding your comfort zone, you will expand the size of your income and wealth zone. The more comfortable you have to be, the fewer risks you will be willing to take, the fewer opportunities you will take advantage of, the fewer people you will meet, and the fewer new strategies you will try. …The more comfort becomes your priority, the more contracted you become with fear."

About three years ago, I decided to get back into the real estate investing field. I had been out of it for 10 years. Before I could buy another property, I had to confront my fears and my comfort zone. I had gotten comfortable outside of the risks of real estate investing. Buying a foreclosed property and rehabbing it has its own inherent risks. I wondered if I could locate good contractors to help me, whether I would be able to get good tenants again, and whether I could handle all of the "unexpected" things that inevitably arise.

I confronted my fears and plunged in. It was uncomfortable at first. But in the end, I grew tremendously and have been able to acquire several pieces of real estate and again create profits for my household.

Another thing that Eker says is that "The only time you are actually growing is when you are uncomfortable." I believe that. We can never expand ourselves by continuing to only do what is comfortable. We have to try new activities, learn something new, and move in a new direction in order to continue growing.

A Poverty Mindset Causes Waste

When you have a poverty mindset, you not only will live in lack, but you will waste whatever excess resources come your way. The reason is because your mind has been set for poverty, it is uncomfortable with prosperity so it finds a way to get rid of any excess money. That is the main reason why most people with a poverty mindset find it difficult to save money.

Jason (not his real name) was fortunate enough to inherit a large sum of money when a relative died. However, Jason had a poverty mindset and could not handle that large increase in income. His family members encouraged him to save some of it for retirement, but he did not listen. He bought a lot of toys – a new car, some fancy clothes, went on a vacation. He even loaned a large sum to an irresponsible friend who, of course, never paid him back.

After a few years of spending and living for the moment, Jason was flat broke. He not only had wasted his inheritance, but he had also lost his home and job. His poverty mindset caused him to squander his sudden wealth and brought the poverty that he was comfortable with in his mind.

People may say that they want to be wealthy. However, a mindset that is set for poverty cannot handle a sudden increase in wealth. We see this same thing happen over and over again to lottery winners. They will win millions of dollars in the lottery but then a few years later, they have lost it all, are in bankruptcy and many times are worst off financially than they were before they won the millions.

On a smaller scale, you see people in households who can never seem to save any money. Money is wasted on little insignificant things. I often tell people, it is not the $1000 decisions that wreck your budget; it is usually the $5 and $10 decisions that keep you from getting ahead. Most people think if something only costs $5 or $10, it's not a big deal so they go ahead and buy it. But when you add up those small decisions over the course of a week or a month, it ends up being hundreds and hundreds of dollars wasted.

Because of the poverty mindset, you never set up a written budget to plan the use of your finances. You never set financial goals for what you want your money to accomplish. You just let it flow through your fingers and out of your pocket and the end result is being broke.

You have to make a decision that you want to stop wasting the resources that God has entrusted you to manage. Learn about budgeting and getting out of debt. In my first book, Stop Robbing Peter to Pay Paul, I have several forms and charts that can be used to help you set up and stick with a budget. I also give tons of ideas and strategies designed to take the stress out of managing your money. Make your money matter. Even if your income is not as high as you would like for it to be, you can accomplish more with financial goals and a written plan to accomplish them.

Ignorance Keeps You Broke

The Bible says in Hosea 4:6, “My people are destroyed for lack of knowledge.” I hear so many people lament, “I am not good with money.” And they just accept that statement as a fact. No one is born a financial expert and wiz. Although some people may have a knack for handling money, they still have to develop the ability in order to manage money well.

Unfortunately, we do a horrible job in educating people on how to manage money. Our educational system teaches knowledge, and specialized skills in order to obtain a job. But rarely do you find a course in Household Budgeting being taught.

If you want to be an excellent steward of the financial resources that God has blessed you with, then it is imperative that you take the time to learn how to manage your money. Read a good book, take a class, or go to a workshop. Learn not just about managing money and budgeting but also about tithing, giving, investing and growing your money.

First and foremost, we need to study God’s Word on the topic of money. There are over 2,250 scriptures that deal with money in the Bible. In fact, there are more scriptures in the Bible on money than there are on faith and prayer. God has written these scriptures to help us gain wisdom in managing money as a valuable tool for the kingdom. In later chapters, we will be expounding on what the Word of God teaches on money and prosperity in greater detail.

Complaining and Criticizing Brings Lack

Have you ever known someone who every time you see them they are complaining about one problem after another. First, it's their job that is causing them a problem, then they complain because the car broke down, or the kids are being unruly, or it's the spouse whose getting on their nerves. And on and on it goes.

People who complain all the time end up criticizing themselves, their circumstances and others. Often, they blame others for their situation. It is always someone else's fault – their spouse, their boss, their children, the economy or simply bad luck. The problem with complaining and criticizing is that it demonstrates a lack of gratitude and a sense of pride.

In Isaiah 58, the people were complaining to God that He hadn't noticed their fasting and hadn't provided the blessings they sought by doing so. God let them know that it was something more important to Him than mere fasting.

Isaiah 58:3-9

[3]'Why have we fasted,' they say, 'and You have not seen? Why have we afflicted our souls, and You take no notice?' "In fact, in the day of your fast you find pleasure, and exploit all your laborers.

[4]Indeed you fast for strife and debate, and to strike with the fist of wickedness. You will not fast as you do this day, to make your voice heard on high.

[5]Is it a fast that I have chosen, a day for a man to afflict his soul? Is it to bow down his head like a bulrush, and to spread out sackcloth and ashes? Would you call this a fast, and an acceptable day to the LORD?

> [6]"Is this not the fast that I have chosen: to loose the bonds of wickedness, to undo the heavy burdens, to let the oppressed go free, and that you break every yoke?
> [7]Is it not to share your bread with the hungry, and that you bring to your house the poor who are cast out; when you see the naked, that you cover him, and not hide yourself from your own flesh?
> [8]Then your light shall break forth like the morning, your healing shall spring forth speedily, and your righteousness shall go before you; the glory of the LORD shall be your rear guard.
> [9]Then you shall call, and the LORD will answer; you shall cry, and He will say, 'Here I am.' "*If you take away the yoke from your midst, the pointing of the finger, and speaking wickedness.* (Emphasis added)

God was not pleased with the fasting of the Israelites because their attitude was not right. It had become a legalistic competition among the people. They were complaining, criticizing one another and pointing fingers of blame. These bad attitudes caused God to withhold His blessings from them.

God let them know in verse eight, that if they fasted and prayed with the right attitude, then all of their needs would be met. Healing would be theirs; their righteousness would open doors for them and God's glory would protect them from their enemies. God will answer our prayers when we have the right attitude in our hearts.

"There is possibly nothing that can so radically change the church, and the lives of individual believers, than having the critical spirit removed from our midst. The best way to remove it is to have our criticisms changed into intercession. The Lord lives to intercede, while the devil lives to accuse," says Rick Joyner in Overcoming the Spirit of Poverty.

Criticizing others is very dangerous because it puts you in a position of looking down on someone else. It comes from a spirit of pride. There are many verses of scripture that speak against pride in the book of wisdom, Proverbs. "In the mouth of the foolish is a rod of pride: but the lips of the wise shall preserve them. (Chapter 14:3)" "A man's pride shall bring him low: but honour shall uphold the humble in spirit. (Chapter 29:23)" "Pride goeth before destruction, and an haughty spirit before a fall. (Chapter 16:18)"

If we want the blessings of God to flow in our lives, stop complaining and criticizing and start praying and giving thanks. The attitude of your heart is important to God.

Laziness Will Cause You to Be Broke

You cannot be lazy and expect to walk in the prosperity that God has for your life. We all know the story of the parable of the talents in Matthew 25. A rich man gave a sum of money to each of three servants. One servant received five talents, the second one got two talents and the third one got one talent. A talent was a form of currency in Biblical days. The first two servants invested their lord's money and doubled it by the time he returned.

However, the third servant hid his one talent in the ground. His reason for hiding the talent gives a clue as to his spirit of laziness that eventually brought him to poverty. "Then he who had received the one talent came and said, 'Lord, I knew you to be a hard man, reaping where you have not sown, and gathering where you have not scattered seed. 'And I was afraid, and went and hid your talent in the ground. Look, there you have what is yours.'" (Matthew 25:24-25)

In the end, the lord took the one talent from this servant and gave it to the one who had ten talents, so he ended up broke. There are three reasons why he ended up broke. First, he was disobedient. Evidently, the other two servants got the memo. You know the memo, which said "Do something productive with my money while I am gone." The disobedient servant didn't get the memo, forgot to read the memo, or more likely, just decided not to obey the command.

Second, the servant was selfish and lazy. He knew that the Lord reaped where He had not sown. So I can only imagine him thinking, "Why should I expend all of my time and effort to produce a profit that I will just have to give to the lord on his return." Hiding the talent in the ground did not require any effort. He was lazy.

Finally, the servant was filled with fear. He told the lord that because he was afraid, he hid the talent in the ground. Debilitating fear that causes you to be paralyzed with inaction comes from satan. He desires to stop you from taking the actions you need to take to bring God's prosperity into your life. Laziness coupled with fear and disobedience caused this servant to end up broke.

Proverbs 6:6-11 says, "Go to the ant, you sluggard! Consider her ways and be wise, which, having no captain, overseer or ruler, provides her supplies in the summer, and gathers her food in the harvest. How long will you slumber, O sluggard? When will you rise from your sleep? A little sleep, a little slumber, a little folding of the hands to sleep – so shall your poverty come on you like a prowler, and your need like an armed man." We need to get rid of laziness if we want God's prosperity in our lives. Laziness brings poverty.

Faithless People Miss the Blessing

Part of the purpose in me writing this book is to build the faith of God's people to receive all that God has for them. We need to stop living in lack, struggling to accomplish God's purpose for our lives. God has all of the resources of the universe at His disposal and is well equipped to release to us whatever we need. But we have to have faith to receive His blessings.

We all know the story of the nation of Israel and how God told them He was giving them the Promised Land. Twelve spies were sent into the land to check it out. When they got to the Promised Land, it was exactly as God had promised. All the spies saw a land flowing with milk and honey; they saw the huge cluster of grapes that required two people to carry it, the pomegranates and the figs of the land. They saw the prosperity that was evident in the land. They saw the beautiful wealth of the real estate – the valleys and the high places.

Joshua and Caleb saw the same things that the other ten saw. In addition to the positive things, they also saw the obstacles that stood in their way. They saw the walls, the fortified cities, the armed forces, the valiant men, and the giants.

Since all the spies saw the same things, the issue was not with what they saw; the problem was in the interpretation of what was seen. The ten spies stumbled at what they saw while Joshua and Caleb rejoiced at what they saw. Too often we miss out on the promises of God because we don't filter what we see through our faith in God's Word. Joshua and Caleb kept God's promise in the forefront of their minds.

Faith sees what evidence doesn't show, that is why Hebrews 11:1 says that faith is "the evidence of things not seen". Faith is not what you see but what you trust God to do despite what you might see. God said that Caleb had a different spirit. We need that type of spirit today that is able to trust God to do what He has promised despite what we may see.

Because the ten spies lacked faith in God's Word, they convinced the people that it would be impossible to fight the giants. The people listened to their faithless report and as a result, they died in the wilderness in a state of poverty. Their lack of faith in God caused them to miss the blessing that God had planned for them. Instead, their children received the blessing.

CHAPTER 2

GODLY AND PROSPEROUS

Most people want the financial prosperity of God to flow in their lives, but few people really understand what it takes to make it happen. The Word of God gives us several key principles that will help financial blessings to manifest in our lives. What does it take to move from praising God in faith for your financial blessings to seeing the manifestation of them? Wisdom is needed in order to produce prosperity. Proverbs 3:13 & 16 says, "Happy is the man who finds wisdom, and the man who gains understanding; Length of days is in her right hand, in her left hand riches and honor.

Seven Keys to Prosperity

Although there are several other principles that I will cover in the chapter on Developing a Prosperous Mindset, I believe there are seven foundational keys to financial success.

Key #1 - Seek God First

God wants to be Lord of our lives, which means He wants to be in charge. We should, therefore, seek God's wisdom for our lives first. We need to spend time in prayer and in the presence of God so He can give us His direction. Before you decide what career to pursue, seek God's wisdom. Before you decide to start that business venture, pray about it. Before you decide to make an impulsive purchase, ask God about it.

Seeking God first needs to become a habit in our lives. Before you do anything else each day, seek God's blessing on your day by spending time in prayer. Seek God before you establish your goals and plans. When you have problems, cry out to God first, before you call your friends for advice.

Key #2 - Obey God

We love to quote parts of Deuteronomy 28, there's even a song we sing about it – we're blessed in the city, we're blessed in the field, we're blessed when we come and when we go. All of this is true. But in order to accurately understand scripture, it is best to read it in its full context.

In Deuteronomy 28:1-2, it says "And it shall come to pass, if thou shalt hearken diligently unto the voice of the LORD thy God, to observe and to do all his commandments which I command thee this day, that the LORD thy God will set thee on high above all nations of the earth: And all these blessings shall come on thee, and overtake thee, if thou shalt hearken unto the voice of the LORD thy God."

There is one small but key word in this verse which is key – that word is "if", which means that the blessings of verses 2-14 are conditional upon obedience to the requirements of verses one and two. Part of the blessing mentioned in verse 12 is that you shall lend to many nations and not borrow, which means that God not only wants us out of debt, but he wants us to have an overflow so that we can bless others.

Key #3 - Tithe Consistently

I have spoken with so many Christians who consider tithing to be optional or dependent upon what bills come in that week. They justify it by saying, "God knows my heart." Yet they continue to expect God's blessing on their finances. In Leviticus 27:30, God decrees that the tithe is holy. When God says something is holy, it means it has been sanctified or set apart for God's use alone. The tithe is to be returned to your local church to meet the needs of that ministry.

When we touch something that God says is holy in the wrong way, it can cause death. When you spend the tithe, it causes death to your finances. Your car breaks down and you don't have money to get it fixed. Or you are always behind the financial eight ball and can never seem to catch up.

Psalms 138:2 says that God has magnified His Word above His name. This means that even God is submitted to His own Word, He cannot violate it! Since the Word says that tithing opens the windows of heaven for God to bless you, if you don't tithe then you have tied God's hands and prevented him from helping you. Tithing releases financial blessings on your life.

Key #4 - Give Generously

The Bible says in II Corinthians 9:6, "He who sows sparingly will also reap sparingly, and he who sows bountifully will also reap bountifully." The principle of sowing and reaping works in many areas of our lives. Whatever we sow – whether it is love, forgiveness or money – that is what we will reap. When we give generously, God takes note of it and causes money to flow in our lives.

We need to give as the Holy Spirit leads to ministries that meet the needs of people, such as homeless shelters, programs for teenage unwed mothers, substance abuse shelters, and soul-winning ministries that help people find deliverance and hope in Jesus Christ. When we do, we will reap a financial harvest.

Key #5 - Get Out of Debt

In Deuteronomy 28:44, being in debt is listed under the curses for disobedience to God. God's desire is for us to have an overflow so that we can meet all the needs of our household and have excess that we can use to bless others. While God does not say in His Word that we should never go into debt, it does give instructions on paying off debts as soon as possible. It was never God's intention for us to be perpetually in debt.

When you are in debt, you are actually in bondage, according to Proverbs 22:7, "The rich rules over the poor, and the borrower is servant to the lender." Your creditor is actually your taskmaster because he has the right to tell you to go to work whether you want to or not. He may even tell you to get a part-time job or work overtime so you can pay off your bills.

You may feel the call of God on your life to go into full-time ministry, but because you are in debt, you cannot go. Your creditors are demanding that you pay them and if you don't they can haul you into court and get a judgment against you and garnishee your wages to force you to pay them. They are your taskmasters.

To fully participate in the blessings of God, we need to walk away from the curses by getting out of debt. In my book, Stop Robbing Peter to Pay Paul, I give a step-by-step plan of action for how to get out of debt. The book is available online at www.StopRobbingPeter.com.

Key #6 - Get in Position

We need to be in the right position to receive God's prosperity. The right position means being in the right place at the right time so the blessings of God can flow in your life. God designed you for a specific purpose that only you can fulfill. When you have discovered your purpose and are operating in it, then God's financial resources will flow to you to allow you to fulfill your assignment.

There is also a divine timing to your life. The Bible says in Ecclesiastes 3:1, "To every thing there is a season and a time to every purpose under the heaven." We need to always be sensitive to the leading of the Holy Spirit so that we will know our season. To go forward in your purpose before your divine timing can bring destruction; to go forward in your purpose after your timing can cause you to miss your season all together.

Key #7 - Work Diligently

God will give you an assignment, along with the anointing, ability and resources to accomplishment it, however, he will not do the work for you. Some people act as if all we have to do as Christians is to confess God's promises over our lives and then they will come to pass. God is no longer raining manna from heaven; he expects us to work hard.

Proverbs 13:4 says, "The soul of a lazy man desires, and has nothing; but the soul of the diligent shall be made rich." You cannot be lazy and expect to have financial success. God expects us to work hard, be diligent, faithful and consistent, and then we will see the manifestation of our financial blessing.

Examples of Godly Prosperity

The Word of God gives us examples of people who were servants of God, who feared God, walked in integrity and had great faith in God's ability to provide for their financial needs. We can learn about God's desire to prosper His people by examining their stories.

The Widow Woman – Her Faith Brought Prosperity

The widow in II Kings 4:1-7 had a problem that unfortunately is all too common today as well. Her husband had died and left some unpaid bills. In those days, however, the creditors had the right to put her sons in prison to compensate them for the money that was owed. In desperation, the widow cried out to the prophet Elisha for assistance.

Elisha asked her an interesting question, "What's in your house?" In other words, what has God already given to you that you can use to bring your financial increase? The only thing the widow had in her house was a pot of oil, which she probably did not think was all that special. The prophet then instructed her to borrow a lot of vessels from all of her neighbors. Once she gathered the vessels, she shut herself up in the house and began to pour oil from her one pot into the vessels she borrowed. God supernaturally multiplied her oil to fill every vessel she borrowed. Once she ran out of vessels, the oil stopped flowing. Elisha then instructed her to go and sell the vessels of oil, use the profits to pay back all of her husband's debts and to live comfortably off the rest of the profits.

The widow's experience teaches us several principles for financial blessings. First, the level of her faith determined the level of her blessing. When the prophet told her to borrow some vessels, he did not tell her how many, he just said, 'don't borrow a few'. When the prophet told her to borrow the vessels, he also did not tell her what was going to happen. She had to borrow the vessels in faith. The scripture doesn't tell us how many vessels she actually borrowed. We don't know if it was 20 or 50 or 500 or 1000. But we do know that every vessel she borrowed was filled with oil.

Likewise, God has designed each of us to fulfill a unique purpose in the earth. If we seek His face, He will guide us in terms of what profession or vocation to pursue. He may even speak to our hearts about starting a business venture. When we hear from God, we need to immediately obey Him in faith. We have to take the steps in the natural through diligent hard work, getting to work on time, being faithful and loyal in the tasks we are assigned. The level of our faith will determine how passionately we pursue what God has told us to do.

The second principle we learn from the widow is that whatever you need is already in your house. God has blessed each of us with gifts, skills and abilities so we can live out our destiny. Someone may have the "hobby" of home decorating. God may want you to use that ability to start a business venture that will not only bless the lives of others but also create an income for your family. When we use what we already have, it allows God to bless us financially through using our gifts and abilities to serve the needs of others.

The final principle the widow teaches us is that when we obey God in the natural, He will move supernaturally on our behalf so our financial blessing can be released. The one pot of oil that the widow had was not enough to meet her needs, but when she released her faith by obeying God, borrowing vessels and filling them with oil, then God could move supernaturally on her behalf to bring her financial increase. Likewise, when we take action in faith in obedience to the Word of God for our life, we can also have faith to expect supernatural blessings on our efforts.

To release our financial blessings, we need to have faith, take action based on God's leading, and expect God to provide the supernatural increase!

David – Faithfulness Led to Prosperity

After God rejected Saul as king over Israel for his disobedience, He instructed the prophet Samuel to anoint David as the next king of the nation of Israel. Samuel went to the home of Jesse of Bethlehem. Jesse had eight sons and David was his youngest. David was not initially thought of by his father as suitable to be king as Jesse had his seven other sons pass by Samuel first. When Samuel saw David, the Lord told Samuel to anoint David as the next king of Israel. Although David did not immediately take over the throne, the anointing of the Holy Spirit came on him from that point on. David did not have a high position; he was a shepherd but he was faithful in his job (I Samuel 16:11). His faithfulness in natural responsibilities may have been one of the qualities that qualified him for his spiritual assignment.

As a shepherd, David's job required his 24-hour, 7 day a week attention. In the natural, a shepherd is a very hard working, caring, sleepless, kind person who loves his flock. A shepherd knows each of his sheep by name. Another quality of a good shepherd is that he is the door for the sheep. In the natural, a sheep pen has no physical door. At night, after the shepherd has made sure that all of the sheep are in the pen, he lies down at the entrance and becomes a human door. No sheep can get out without crossing him and no predator can get in without crossing him. If necessary, a shepherd will fight a predator at times giving his life to save the life of his sheep. David learned fighting skills while protecting his sheep; he slew both lions and bears that tried to attack the sheep (I Samuel

17:34-36). While being a shepherd, David also exemplified great faith in God. He acknowledged that it was God who delivered him from the bear and lion (I Samuel 17:37).

David was obedience to those in authority over him. He quickly obeyed his father without gripping or complaining. How we respond to earthly authority figures is usually indicative of how we respond to God. If we are quick to obey our earthly parents, we will usually be quick to obey our heavenly Father as well. David's obedient nature allowed God to use him mightily later and helped bring his prosperity.

Jesse asked his son to take food to his brothers who were camped out fighting the Philistines in the Valley of Elah (I Samuel 17:17-19). No only did David go quickly, but he showed great care, responsibility and maturity as he went.

In I Samuel 17:20-22 says "So David rose early in the morning, left the sheep with a keeper, and took the things and went as Jesse had commanded him. And he came to the camp as the army was going out to the fight and shouting for the battle. For Israel and the Philistines had drawn up in battle array, army against army. And David left his supplies in the hand of the supply keeper, ran to the army, and came and greeted his brothers."

In handling his father's request, David did not sleep in or waste time, he got up early. He was responsible for his sheep and made sure that they were properly cared for by a keeper before he left. David took care of all the details. When he got to the battleground, he left all of his supplies with a keeper before running off to greet his brothers in the battle. These positive characteristics of responsibility, care and maturity were a great benefit to David.

When David heard the boasting of the giant Philistine, Goliath, he was appalled that the army was running scared from him! "Then David spoke to the men who stood by him, saying, 'what shall be done for the man who kills this Philistine and takes away the reproach from Israel? For who is this uncircumcised Philistine, that he should defy the armies of the living God?'" (I Samuel 17:26) Because of David's great faith in God, his courage, and his experience in fighting off animals that attacked his sheep, he had faith in God to believe he could destroy Goliath. He felt the giant taunting of the Israelite troops was a disgrace to the power of Almighty God.

David not only displayed faith but also great boldness as he approached Goliath. He told the giant that he was coming after him "in the name of the Lord of Hosts". His great faith and boldness was followed with action as he slew Goliath with a slingshot. These qualities were a tremendous help to the nation of Israel as his victory restored confidence in the rest of the troops. After Goliath was dead, they were able to pursue and overtake the rest of the Philistine army, plundering all of their valuables. David was rewarded with wealth from King Saul, his daughter Michal as his wife and a new job as Saul's armor bearer.

David knew the importance of covenant as he established a covenant relationship with Saul's son, Jonathan. This friendship was a true God-given bond that proved to be tremendously beneficial for David as Jonathan gave him advanced warning when Saul turned on David. David honored this covenant even after Jonathan's death as he found Jonathan's son, Mephibosheth, to show kindness and favor to because of that covenant (II Samuel 9:1-6).

As armor bearer for King Saul, David exemplified respect for the position that God had placed Saul in and wisdom that allowed him to protect himself from Saul's jealous attacks on him. When an evil spirit tormented Saul, David played his harp to soothe him. Because David had slew Goliath, his fame spread rapidly. The women began to sing a song of victory acknowledging that Saul had killed thousands but that David had killed ten thousands (I Samuel 18:6-7). Saul was infuriated that he was not getting top billing and in a jealous rage threw a javelin at David. Saul knew that the anointing of God had departed from him and suspected that David was in line to take over the throne.

Saul's jealousy of David led him to issue an order to have David killed. But since David had a covenant with Saul's son, Jonathan, he was able to get favor and an advance warning. God protected David from Saul's attacks three times. Although David was presented with an opportunity to kill Saul when he went into a cave that David was hiding in, David did not kill him but only cut off a corner of his garment so he could show Saul that he was not a threat to his kingdom. David lived the verse in Psalms 105:15, which says, "Touch not mine anointed, and do my prophets no harm." He saw Saul as the God-anointed king of Israel and refused to harm him.

As David fled from Saul's pursuit, he went to a cave in Adullam. Because of the respect he had garnered from the people, a lot of men followed him there. In fact, the crowd that followed him included a bunch of downcast people who had problems! "And every one that was in distress, and every one that was in debt, and every one that was discontented, gathered themselves unto him; and he became a captain over them: and there were with him about four hundred men." (I Samuel 22:2)

The Bible doesn't record all of the issues and drama that must have ensued after these men arrived but it had to be a lot. All of these men were either in distress, in debt or discontent, not exactly a happy crowd to be around! However, because David had learned leadership skills while taking care of sheep and warrior skills while fighting for the nation of Israel, he was able to teach and train these 400 men to become an army of mighty men.

David again exemplified his dynamic relationship with God as his leader when he inquired of God whether he was to take his mighty men and go fight the Philistines to save the city of Keilah. David did not take it upon himself to decide what to do but he sought God's wisdom and direction at every turn. God told him to go and fight the battle and David and his mighty men were successful and saved the inhabitants of Keilah (I Samuel 23:1-5). David fought many more battles with God granting him victory over all of his enemies.

After David became king over the nation of Israel, his war conquests gave the nation great pride as he defeated enemies, took over Jerusalem and made Israel into a world power to be respected by the nations surrounding it. Every time David won a battle, he also plundered his enemies and brought back gold, silver, flocks, herds, clothing and other goods. In other words, he became a very wealthy man. But his wealth was not acquired overnight or instantaneously. His wealth was the result of years of pursuing God, exercising his faith in God, working hard, being responsible and becoming the leader God called him to be.

Joseph – Prosperity to Save a Nation

Joseph endured a lot of hardship and abuse but God used all of his experiences to bring him to a place of prosperity for the purpose of saving an entire nation from destruction.

Godly and Prosperous

As a teenager, Joseph dreamed prophetically, which showed that his brothers and parents would one day bow down to him. Probably out of immaturity, he proudly shared these dreams with his siblings. Joseph was also Jacob's favorite child since he was born by the wife he loved, Rachel. These two factors ignited jealousy and rage in Joseph's brother who then plotted to kill him but instead threw him into a cistern, sold him as a slave to Egypt and told their father that a wild animal had killed him.

Instead of becoming bitter and resentful due to the horrible treatment he had received, Joseph focused his life on seeking God and fulfilling his purpose. Joseph's godly fear and obedience helped lead him to a place of prosperity. To fear God means to have a reverence and respect for God as the sovereign supreme authority of life. Joseph displayed this fear of the Lord in all that he did.

Once in Egypt, he excelled to a position in Potiphar's house of second in command. The Lord made all that he did to prosper in his hand. With Joseph in the land of Egypt, we see God using prosperity as a tool for witness. We read here that Joseph's master realized that the Lord was with him in everything he did, and that it prospered in his hand. (Genesis 39:2-6). However, after Potiphar's wife falsely accused Joseph of trying to seduce her, he found himself in jail for a crime he did not commit.

Again, instead of becoming bitter, Joseph chose to glorify God in the prison and God allowed him to be placed in a leadership role while in jail. The Lord was with Joseph and the warden granted him favor to be placed in charge of the prison (Genesis 39:20-23). God used Joseph in prison to interpret dreams of a baker and a butler. Because of Joseph's obedience to God to give the interpretations, it proved to be a turning point to his eventual promotion.

When the butler was released from prison and remembered Joseph's ability to interpret dreams, Joseph obtained his freedom because the Pharaoh had some troubling dreams that he needed to be interpreted. Joseph correctly told Pharaoh that the dreams foretold seven years of plenty followed by seven years of famine. Recognizing the wisdom of God on Joseph, Pharaoh placed him in a position as second-in-command in Egypt.

Genesis 41:39-44
39Then Pharaoh said to Joseph, "Inasmuch as
God has shown you all this, there is no one
as discerning and wise as you.
40"You shall be over my house, and all my
people shall be ruled according to your
word; only in regard to the throne will I be
greater than you."
41And Pharaoh said to Joseph, "See, I have
set you over all the land of Egypt."
42Then Pharaoh took his signet ring off his
hand and put it on Joseph's hand; and he
clothed him in garments of fine linen and
put a gold chain around his neck.
43And he had him ride in the second chariot
which he had; and they cried out before him,
"Bow the knee!" So he set him over all the
land of Egypt.
44Pharaoh also said to Joseph, "I am
Pharaoh, and without your consent no man
may lift his hand or foot in all the land of
Egypt.

Because of his life of faithfulness, commitment and integrity, Joseph was promoted to a position of great wealth. He had the job of managing all of the grain that was produced during the seven years of plenty so that enough would be stored up to provide for the seven years of famine that would follow. Joseph was a man of vision. All great leaders have vision and are able to inspire their followers to believe in and help fulfill the vision. Through God's revelation, Joseph saw the feast and famine periods that were coming upon Egypt and he was able to set up a system of food storage and rationing which saved a nation and his people from starvation (Genesis 41:46-49,55-57).

Joseph's prosperity was part of a bigger plan. God didn't prosper Joseph just for the sake of Joseph; he blessed him so that his family would all be spared. We can never see prosperity as an end in itself; God blesses us to become a blessing. When Joseph's brothers came to buy grain, Joseph was in a position where he could have exacted revenge upon them but instead he showed them compassion and sold them the grain. Later, when Joseph wanted to bring his family down to Egypt, as second-in-command, he had the "best of Egypt" available to him to give to his family (Genesis 45:19-20).

Joseph wasn't seeking prosperity; he was seeking God. So many times we can get the prosperity message backwards. We want to prosper, or be successful, so that we can glorify God: but the truth is, we should seek God's glory, so that He might make us to prosper. Deuteronomy 29:9 says, "Therefore keep the words of this covenant, and do them, that you may prosper in all that you do."

The Nation of Israel
Overnight Wealth to Worship God

The nation of Israel spent over 400 years in bondage in Egypt. During this time period Egypt became one of the wealthiest nations on the earth. Pharaoh and

Egypt were the superpower of that day. God allowed Egypt to prosper during the 400 years of Israel's slavery because their wealth was being accumulated so it could be transferred supernaturally to God's chosen people.

When God told Moses to lead them out of bondage, it was so that the people could serve God, worship Him and build a tabernacle to worship Him in. As slaves, they didn't own anything and were at the mercy of their taskmasters. However, God knew that they would need financial resources in order the make their journey and accomplish his purpose.

In order to obtain the resources needed to build the tabernacle, God told Moses what to have the people do prior to the last plague of death of the firstborn being placed on Egypt. He provided the children of Israel with a supernatural wealth transfer.

> **Exodus 3:21-22**
> 21 And I will give this people favor in the sight of the Egyptians; and it shall be, when you go, that you shall not go empty-handed.
>
> 22 But every woman shall ask of her neighbor, namely, of her who dwells near her house, articles of silver, articles of gold, and clothing; and you shall put them on your sons and on your daughters. So you shall plunder the Egyptians.
>
> **Exodus 12:33-36**
> 33 And the Egyptians urged the people, that they might send them out of the land in haste. For they said, "We shall all be dead."

34So the people took their dough before it
was leavened, having their kneading bowls
bound up in their clothes on their shoulders.
35Now the children of Israel had done
according to the word of Moses, and they
had asked from the Egyptians articles of
silver, articles of gold, and clothing.
36And the LORD had given the people favor
in the sight of the Egyptians, so that they
granted them what they requested. Thus they
plundered the Egyptians.

As a result of the Israelites plundering the Egyptians of their gold and silver and Pharaoh's unwise decision to pursue the Israelites that caused the drowning of Egypt's army in the Red Sea, Egypt was utterly destroyed. It was both financially and militarily bankrupt and never recovered its status as a superpower.

Later, when God gave Moses instructions to build a sanctuary, He required the people to bring an offering in order for the sanctuary to be built. The Israelites were able to bring all of these precious things to God as an offering because they had gotten them from the Egyptians.

Exodus 25:2-8
2Speak to the children of Israel, that they
bring Me an offering. From everyone who
gives it willingly with his heart you shall
take My offering.
3And this is the offering which you shall
take from them: gold, silver, and bronze;
4blue, purple, and scarlet thread, fine linen,
and goats' hair;

[5]ram skins dyed red, badger skins, and acacia wood;
[6]oil for the light, and spices for the anointing oil and for the sweet incense;
[7]onyx stones, and stones to be set in the ephod and in the breastplate.
[8]And let them make Me a sanctuary, that I may dwell among them.

The Five-Talent Servant
Effective Stewardship Produced Wealth

The parable of the talents in the Bible is one of my favorite scriptures for teaching financial stewardship because it gives us so many valuable lessons. We can learn how to be prosperous from the servants who received five and two talents. And we learn how to be broke from the servant who received one talent.

Matthew 25:14-16
[14]For the kingdom of heaven is like a man traveling to a far country, who called his own servants and delivered his goods to them.
[15]And to one he gave five talents, to another two, and to another one, to each according to his own ability; and immediately he went on a journey.
[16]Then he who had received the five talents went and traded with them, and made another five talents.

Some people like to spiritualize this passage to say that it only applies to use of your natural talents or spiritual gifts for service in the church. However, I believe we can learn principles for handling money from a literal review of this passage.

During biblical days, a talent was a form of currency. One denarius equaled a day's wages. One talent equaled 6,000 denari. Since the Israelites worked six days a week, one talent would pay them for 1,000 weeks of work If you compute the math, then one talent was the equivalent of 20 years of wages lump sum. The person with two talents received the equivalent of 40 years of wages and the person with five talents received an equivalent of 100 years of wages lump sum to manage. If you were to convert this to U.S. wages using an average income of $40,000 per year, for example, then the one-talent person received the equivalent of $800,000 to manage, the two-talent person got $1.6 million and the five-talent person got $4 million! Even the person who was given only one talent was still given a lot of money to manage. If you were given that much money at one time, could you handle it?

I went through all the trouble to compute these numbers because some people say that you can only find wealthy people in the Old Testament of the Bible and no evidence that God wants us to manage large sums of money in the New Testament. Well, I believe the parable of the talents shows that God is willing to bless us with large sums of money but there are conditions.

The first principle we glean from this passage is that God is the owner and we are managers. The Lord put each individual in charge of managing a portion of His assets. We are stewards or managers of God's money; it doesn't belong to us.

A second principle, which is key to understanding prosperity today, is that God gave money to each individual *according to his ability to handle it*. Not everyone is going to be given the same amount of money to manage. One person was given five talents; another two and the last person was given one talent. Some people are given more money because they are more faithful and skilled in handling it. If you want God to bless you with an increase in income, become more skilled and faithful in handling the amount of money that you have right now.

Matthew 25:19-21
19 After a long time the lord of those servants came and settled accounts with them.
20 So he who had received five talents came and brought five other talents, saying, 'Lord, you delivered to me five talents; look, I have gained five more talents besides them.'
21 His lord said to him, 'Well done, good and faithful servant; you were faithful over a few things, I will make you ruler over many things. Enter into the joy of your lord.'

Another principle we can learn from this passage is that as owner of our money, God has the right to review our use of money. What if God came to you and said, "Okay, show me your checkbook, your bank statements and your charge card statements, it's time to do an audit!" Many of us shriek at the very thought of that! But since we are only managers of God's assets, we need to constantly remind ourselves that we are accountable to Him for what we do with what He has provided for us.

This parable also teaches us that God expects multiplication of our finances and not just maintenance. The Lord was pleased with the person who was given five talents and the person who was given two talents because both were able to double His money. God expects us to make wise financial decisions that will bless the house of God, while providing for our family today and for generations to come. Proverbs 13:22 (NIV) says, "A good man leaves an inheritance for his children's children, but a sinner's wealth is stored up for the righteous."

Matthew 25:24-29
24 Then he who had received the one talent came and said, 'Lord, I knew you to be a hard man, reaping where you have not sown, and gathering where you have not scattered seed.
25 'And I was afraid, and went and hid your talent in the ground. Look, there you have what is yours.'
26 But his lord answered and said to him, 'You wicked and lazy servant, you knew that I reap where I have not sown, and gather where I have not scattered seed.
27 'So you ought to have deposited my money with the bankers, and at my coming I would have received back my own with interest.
28 Therefore take the talent from him, and give it to him who has ten talents.
29 'For to everyone who has, more will be given, and he will have abundance; but from him who does not have, even what he has will be taken away.

The one individual who hid the money in the earth and did not earn any interest on the money, the Lord was not pleased with him. In fact, the Lord said he was wicked and lazy. The Lord took away his one talent and gave it to the person who started out with five talents.

The person with one talent ended up flat broke. I believe there are three reasons why he ended up broke. First, he was disobedient. The other two servants got the message that the Lord wanted them to invest His money, the one-talent servant refused to obey that command. Second, he was selfish and lazy. He didn't want to work hard so his Lord would reap the benefits. Finally, he allowed fear to stop him from doing anything. I believe the one-talent person's story is prophetic in that it lets us know that there will be some people in the body of Christ who will end up broke as well. People who are disobedient, selfish, lazy and filled with fear will end up broke.

The final principle we learn from the parable of the talents is that if you want to be promoted to the next level in your finances, you need to prove your faithfulness at your current level. The five-talent person multiplied his Lord's money and was commended for doing so. He also received a bonus: the lazy servant's one talent was taken from him and given to the more faithful servant. When we are faithful over a few things, God will make us ruler over many things.

CHAPTER 3

WHERE IS YOUR FAITH?

If you are having a financial challenge, it's easy to fall prey to fear. Bills begin to pile up, creditors start to harass you and you may feel like you are bombarded by negative news. Job layoffs, company closings, white-collar fraud and stock market losses make the daily news. At times the weight of the negative news becomes overwhelming.

It causes fear to mount because the very basis of our financial security is threatened with ongoing negative financial news. Our financial foundations are being shaken. Hebrews 12:27 says, "Now this, yet once more, indicates the removal of those things that are being shaken, as of things that are made, that the things which cannot be shaken may remain."

The things being shaken are those things that we have placed our security in other than God. Our income, employer, net worth, or investment account balance should not be the basis of our security. When these things are threatened, we begin to see the flaw of placing our security in these unstable things to begin with.

Through economic challenges, God is looking for revival. Amos 8:11 says, "Behold, the days are coming, says the Lord GOD, that I will send a famine on the land, not a famine of bread, nor a thirst for water, but of hearing the words of the LORD." There is a famine in the land. Although it may appear to be an economic famine, God is using this experience to show us that we should not just thirst for bread and water or finances and material things but we need to thirst for a word from God.

God desires to speak to His people on a regular basis. He wants us to seek His guidance daily as we live our lives. When times are good, we may stray from God's leading and simply "let the good times roll". However, financial challenges force us to seek God's face. We need His wisdom to make decisions for our households. Should you change jobs or stay where you are? After a job layoff, should you look for a similar job or change fields? Should you relocate to another city? What changes should you make in your investments?

These tough questions require wisdom to find the answers that will fit your unique situation. God alone is the source of true wisdom. Proverbs 4:7 says, "Wisdom is the principal thing; therefore get wisdom. And in all your getting, get understanding." Fortunately, wisdom is readily available when we seek it from God. James 1:5 says, "If any of you lacks wisdom, let him ask of God, who gives to all liberally and without reproach, and it will be given to him."

God wants us to return to dependence on Him as our source. We should be crying out Abba, Father. He is our heavenly father, our loving guardian who seeks to meet all of our needs according to His riches in glory by Christ Jesus. God desires to meet your needs even during times of economic downturns. But you have to have a relationship with God and be willing to hear and respond to His leading.

God Provides For His Own Supernaturally

The prophet Elijah had prayed that there would be no rain and as a result, there was a drought in the land. Since Elijah was the prophet of God, he was totally dependent on God to lead him and feed him during this time.

Where is Your Faith?

I Kings 17:1-16
[1]And Elijah the Tishbite, of the inhabitants of
Gilead, said to Ahab, "As the LORD God of Israel
lives, before whom I stand, there shall not be dew
nor rain these years, except at my word."
[2]Then the word of the LORD came to him, saying,
[3]"Get away from here and turn eastward, and hide
by the Brook Cherith, which flows into the Jordan.
[4]"And it will be that you shall drink from the brook,
and I have commanded the ravens to feed you
there."
[5]So he went and did according to the word of the
LORD, for he went and stayed by the Brook
Cherith, which flows into the Jordan.
[6]The ravens brought him bread and meat in the
morning, and bread and meat in the evening; and he
drank from the brook.
[7]And it happened after a while that the brook dried
up, because there had been no rain in the land.
[8]Then the word of the LORD came to him, saying,
[9]"Arise, go to Zarephath, which belongs to Sidon,
and dwell there. See, I have commanded a widow
there to provide for you."
[10]So he arose and went to Zarephath. And when he
came to the gate of the city, indeed a widow was
there gathering sticks. And he called to her and said,
"Please bring me a little water in a cup, that I may
drink."
[11]And as she was going to get it, he called to her
and said, "Please bring me a morsel of bread in your
hand."
[12]So she said, "As the LORD your God lives, I do
not have bread, only a handful of flour in a bin, and
a little oil in a jar; and see, I am gathering a couple

> of sticks that I may go in and prepare it for myself and my son, that we may eat it, and die."
> 13 And Elijah said to her, "Do not fear; go and do as you have said, but make me a small cake from it first, and bring it to me; and afterward make some for yourself and your son.
> 14 "For thus says the LORD God of Israel: 'The bin of flour shall not be used up, nor shall the jar of oil run dry, until the day the LORD sends rain on the earth.'"
> 15 So she went away and did according to the word of Elijah; and she and he and her household ate for many days.
> 16 The bin of flour was not used up, nor did the jar of oil run dry, according to the word of the LORD which He spoke by Elijah.

When the drought started, God told Elijah *exactly where to go* so that he would have food and water during the midst of the drought. The Brook Cherith provided the water while ravens delivered bread and meat for his nourishment. While Elijah may have gotten used to this arrangement, God allowed the brook to dry up. In a season of economic uncertainty, you can't get bent out of shape if you lose your job. When that source of income dries up, God is able to provide another one if you look to Him for direction.

God readily provided the direction that Elijah needed. In fact, he had planned in advance for Elijah by speaking to a widow in Zarephath even before Elijah got there. Elijah meets the widow when she is at a point of desperation in her life. The drought has taken its toll of her to the point where she has given up. She is gathering sticks to prepare one last meal for her and her son so they can eat it and die.

The widow had to be a woman of faith because when Elijah asked her to bring him a cup of water in the midst of a drought, she didn't tell him off! Then, after asking for water, the prophet Elijah had the audacity to ask her to make some bread and bring him a piece first. She explained her dire situation to the prophet that she only had a handful of flour for her and her son's last meal. The prophet assured her that if she obeyed the Word of the Lord by honoring the prophet of God first, then her bin of flour would not be used up nor would her jar of oil run out.

As she obeyed the Word of God through the prophet Elijah, she received her miracle. In the midst of the drought, she had provisions for her household. The principle here is clear. You need to be sensitive to hear and obey the voice of God as he tells you what to do and where to work during difficult times. Also, during times of financial strain, it is easy to justify to yourself why you should stop tithing and giving to the Lord's work, but it is better to honor God first and trust Him to multiply what you have left over.

Proverbs 3:9-10 says, "Honor the LORD with your possessions, and with the first fruits of all your increase; so your barns will be filled with plenty, and your vats will overflow with new wine."

Three Levels of Faith

There are three levels of faith that you can operate in at any given moment – no faith, a little faith, or great faith. No faith is the same as a fear of loss. When you have little faith, your faith is mixed with doubts. Great faith is faith so strong that it acts on God's Word alone regardless of the circumstances.

Three Levels of Faith	What it means
No Faith	Fear of Loss
Little Faith	Faith mixed with doubts
Great Faith	Faith that acts on God's Word alone

No Faith

Fear is a tool satan uses to destroy your life. If he can keep you in fear, he will keep you out of faith in God. Fear and faith cannot coexist. If you are in fear, you are not in faith. When you walk in faith, it means you have cast off fear.

In the passage of scripture in Mark 4:35-40, we find the disciples allowing fear to overcome them, causing them to have no faith.

Mark 4:35-40

35 On the same day, when evening had come, He
said to them, "Let us cross over to the other side."
36 Now when they had left the multitude, they took
Him along in the boat as He was. And other little
boats were also with Him.
37 And a great windstorm arose, and the waves beat
into the boat, so that it was already filling.
38 But He was in the stern, asleep on a pillow. And
they awoke Him and said to Him, "Teacher, do you
not care that we are perishing?"
39 Then He arose and rebuked the wind, and said to
the sea, "Peace, be still!" And the wind ceased and
there was a great calm.

> [40]But He said to them, "Why are you so fearful? How is it that you have no faith?"

Jesus had told the disciples they would "cross over to the other side". Jesus had faith in the Word He spoke, so much so that He laid down and went to sleep in the midst of the storm. Now if Jesus had said, "We're going into the middle of the sea to perish in a storm," then the disciples would have had reason to fear. But Jesus said they were going to the other side.

In the middle of the journey, a storm arose causing the disciples to panic in fear. Thinking that they were about to perish in the storm, they woke Jesus up. Jesus calmly rebuked the wind and the waves proclaiming, "Peace be still." Then He asked the disciples why they had *no faith.*

You may be facing a financial storm right now but if you are engulfed with fear, Jesus would ask you why you have *no faith.* As long as you keep looking at the circumstances, you will continue to be in fear, but when you believe and focus your mind on the truth of God's Word, your peace will be restored in the midst of the storm.

Little Faith

Peter displayed a little faith when he walked on the water with Jesus while the disciples were in a storm in Matthew 14:25-31.

> **Matthew 14:25-31**
> [25]Now in the fourth watch of the night Jesus went to them, walking on the sea.
> [26]And when the disciples saw Him walking on the sea, they were troubled, saying, "It is a ghost!" And they cried out for fear.

27But immediately Jesus spoke to them, saying, "Be of good cheer! It is I; do not be afraid."
28And Peter answered Him and said, "Lord, if it is You, command me to come to You on the water."
29So He said, "Come." And when Peter had come down out of the boat, he walked on the water to go to Jesus.
30But when he saw that the wind was boisterous, he was afraid; and beginning to sink he cried out, saying, "Lord, save me!"
31And immediately Jesus stretched out His hand and caught him, and said to him, "O you of little faith, why did you doubt?"

Unlike the other disciples who had no faith at all, Peter did exemplify some faith by walking on the water to Jesus. However, when you only have a little faith, it means your faith is mixed with doubts. A little faith can keep you afloat for a season, however, as soon as the circumstances get more dismal, you allow doubts to drown out your faith.

As long as Peter kept his eyes on Jesus and focused on the word Jesus said to him, which was “Come”, then Peter was fine. Even though the storm had not dissipated, he was at peace and making progress in the midst of the storm. But as soon as Peter took his eyes off of Jesus and began looking at the wind, the waves and the storm, he began to sink.

Faith requires us to be led by the Spirit and not be swayed by our physical senses. When we focus on what we can see, hear, smell, touch or taste, our flesh is leading us and not our faith. Peter’s little faith got him out of the boat and walking on water. The eleven disciples who remained in the boat had no faith at that time.

In the midst of a financial challenge, it is easy to look at the circumstances – lost income and unpaid bills – but faith requires you to focus on God as the source of your provision. God has promised to meet all of your needs. Faith requires you to believe that truth regardless of the circumstances.

Great Faith

Beyond no faith and a little faith, there is a level called great faith. The centurion displayed great faith in Jesus when his son was sick in Matthew 8:5-10.

> **Matthew 8:5-10**
> 5 Now when Jesus had entered Capernaum, a
> centurion came to Him, pleading with Him,
> 6 saying, "Lord, my servant is lying at home
> paralyzed, dreadfully tormented."
> 7 And Jesus said to him, "I will come and heal him."
> 8 The centurion answered and said, "Lord, I am not
> worthy that You should come under my roof. But
> only speak a word, and my servant will be healed.
> 9 "For I also am a man under authority, having
> soldiers under me. And I say to this one, 'Go,' and
> he goes; and to another, 'Come,' and he comes; and
> to my servant, 'Do this,' and he does it."
> 10 When Jesus heard it, He marveled, and said to
> those who followed, "Assuredly, I say to you, I
> have not found such great faith, not even in Israel!

Great faith is faith that acts on God's Word alone. When you have great faith, you don't need to get in a prayer line or have hands laid on you to receive a miracle. You would operate like the centurion who told Jesus he needed to only speak a word and his son would be healed.

The centurion understood both the authority of Jesus Christ and the power of his words. A centurion with the Roman army was a captain who had 100 soldiers under his command. He knew the power of his words in the natural. When he gave a command, the soldiers he was over fulfilled that command hastily. He applied that same faith to the word Jesus spoke. He knew Jesus' words had the power within them to bring to pass whatever Jesus said.

The Word of God tells us in Isaiah 55:11, "So shall My word be that goes forth from My mouth; it shall not return to Me void, but it shall accomplish what I please, and it shall prosper in the thing for which I sent it."

God has already spoken His Word regarding how He will care for His people and provide for their needs at all times. He has said, "I have been young, and now am old; yet have I not seen the righteous forsaken, nor his seed begging bread" (Psalms 37:25). He has said, "My God shall supply all your need according to His riches in glory by Christ Jesus" (Philippians 4:19).

Psalms 91 gives us many promises of God's provision and protection during times of calamity. Although others may suffer, God will provide for his children as a loving father.

Psalms 91:1-16

1 He who dwells in the secret place of the Most High shall abide under the shadow of the Almighty.

2 I will say of the LORD, "He is my refuge and my fortress; my God, in Him I will trust."

3 Surely He shall deliver you from the snare of the fowler and from the perilous pestilence.

4 He shall cover you with His feathers, and under His wings you shall take refuge; his truth shall be your shield and buckler.

[5]You shall not be afraid of the terror by night, nor of the arrow that flies by day,
[6]Nor of the pestilence that walks in darkness, nor of the destruction that lays waste at noonday.
[7]A thousand may fall at your side, and ten thousand at your right hand; but it shall not come near you.
[8]Only with your eyes shall you look, and see the reward of the wicked.
[9]Because you have made the LORD, who is my refuge, even the Most High, your dwelling place,
[10]No evil shall befall you, nor shall any plague come near your dwelling;
[11]For He shall give His angels charge over you, to keep you in all your ways.
[12]In their hands they shall bear you up, lest you dash your foot against a stone.
[13]You shall tread upon the lion and the cobra, the young lion and the serpent you shall trample underfoot.
[14]"Because he has set his love upon Me, therefore I will deliver him; I will set him on high, because he has known My name.
[15]He shall call upon Me, and I will answer him; I will be with him in trouble; I will deliver him and honor him.
[16]With long life I will satisfy him, and show him My salvation."

Although we may have financial challenges, we can rest assured as believers that we will not be destroyed. Psalms 91:7 is clear, "A thousand may fall at your side, and ten thousand at your right hand; but it shall not come near you." Trust in God's protection over you and your family.

What Kind of Faith Do You Have

The question is what kind of faith do you have? If you allow fear to engulf you, then you are exhibiting no faith. If you mix your faith with doubts, then you have a little faith. But if you believe and proclaim the Word of God and take action based on God's Word for your life, then you are walking in great faith.

God is the same yesterday, today and forever more. He has not changed. There are many names of God revealed in the scriptures. Each name gives us information about the character of God and His dealings with His people. One of the names of God is Jehovah Jireh, which means "my provider".

God revealed Himself to Abraham as Jehovah Jireh when He told Abraham to offer Isaac to Him as a sacrifice in Genesis 22. Before Abraham could slay his son, God provided a ram in the bush to be sacrificed instead. God provided exactly what Abraham needed at the exact time that he needed it because he had great faith in God. Likewise, when we walk in great faith during our financial challenges, God will provide for our needs as well.

Another name for God is El Shaddai, which means, the Almighty God, the all-sufficient God, or the many-breasted one. As a newborn child gets his nourishment from his mother's breast, we can obtain our nourishment from the breast of God. But God has so many breasts that He is capable of providing much more nourishment than we can ever need. In short, He is the God of more than enough!

Even in times of economic famine, God can not only meet your needs, but He can provide more than what you need so you can have a surplus to use to bless someone else.

Where is Your Faith?

To build your faith, you need to remind yourself of who God is. Confess your faith aloud with this proclamation, "God has not changed. God does not have economic downturns. God is still Jehovah Jireh, my provider. God is still El Shaddai, the God of more than enough. I put my faith in God's Word at all times to do exceedingly abundantly above all that I can ask or think."

CHAPTER 4

SATAN ATTACKS YOUR MIND

God has a divine purpose for your life and He will provide the prosperity you need to accomplish that purpose. However, getting to your destiny is not going to be like a walk in the park. Instead, it will be more like a walk through a minefield, where satan has set traps, hazards and dangers designed to defeat you. One of the main weapons satan uses is to attack your mind.

Joyce Meyer, in her book, Battlefield of the Mind, states, "Satan … attacks your mind, waging war against you on the battlefield of your mind. He wants to overload and overwork your mind by filling it with every kind of wrong thought so it cannot be free and available to the Holy Spirit working through your own human spirit."

Many people allow their minds to think whatever thoughts pop into their heads without evaluating whether those thoughts are beneficial or not. This is a mistake. Your thoughts can affect your emotions, your mood, your actions and ultimately your life overall. So it's imperative that you begin to really listen to your thoughts, make a decision whether or not the thoughts that come in your mind are ones you want to dwell on and discipline your mind to only dwell on godly faith-filled thoughts that will propel you to your destiny.

There are many tools in satan's arsenal that he uses to try to defeat you in your thought life. We will explore some of his tactics in this chapter. By exposing his strategies, you will be able to identify when he is trying to defeat you and gain victory over that situation.

Distraction

The nations of the world today have amassed so many nuclear weapons that people at times worry about the weapons of mass destruction destroying our world. However, despite the proliferation of weaponry in the world, I believe the greater threat on your life right now is satan's weapons of mass *distraction.*

Distraction is one of the principal weapons that satan uses when he attacks your mind. If he can get you off your purpose and consumed with meaningless and frivolous activities, then he has succeeded in defeating you. Or at times, he will distract you with meaningful and good things; however, they may not be the *right* things you need to be doing to take you to your purpose and prosperity.

I'm sure you can relate to this story. There have been many days, where I start off the day with a prioritized list of the things that need to be done. I start working on my top priority item when a phone call comes in with an urgent issue that needs to be addressed. I find myself getting off my priorities and handling this other issue. That issue then leads to another issue and so on until my whole day is gone. My priorities have not been addressed at all. While at times interruptions are unavoidable, we need to discipline our mind to remain focused.

Here's another example that I'm sure you have experienced as well. How many times have you been sitting in church on Sunday morning while the pastor is preaching the Word and you realize that you have no idea what he has said in the past few minutes because your mind has been thinking about something else? This is the enemy causing your mind to be distracted so you miss the Word of God that will change your life. Discipline your mind to be focused so the enemy doesn't defeat you in this area.

Worry and Anxiety

A mind filled with worry and anxiety is a mind that is defeated by satan. Worry causes the mind to go around and around with various "What if?" scenarios. You play out in your mind in vivid details all of the negative things that can possibly happen in your situation. The majority of the time, these negative events never materialize. But satan has defeated you because he has wasted your time and your life by having your mind bound with worry.

Anxiety is a cousin to worry in that it is a state of being fearful and stressed either over present circumstances or over things that may happen in the future. Some people experience anxiety attacks where they are literally immobilized by fear. If you will tune into your thought life during these times, you will find your thoughts are filled with words of dread, doom and gloom.

When you are going through a financial challenge, you will be tempted to worry and fret over your situation. Satan will bombard your thoughts with words like, "You are going to lose everything – your house, your car, your job." "You'll end up broke and on welfare." When these thoughts come, let your mind and satan know that with God, nothing is impossible. God can turn around any situation, even yours.

The Bible tells us in Philippians 4:6, "Be anxious for nothing, but in everything by prayer and supplication, with thanksgiving, let your requests be made known to God." And in 1 Peter 5:7, God tells us to cast all of our cares upon Him. God does not want your mind to be filled with worry and anxiety.

When you worry and are anxious, it inhibits your ability to focus on your God-given assignment. The antidote to worry and anxiety is to learn to pray and trust God with your life and circumstances. When you feel tempted to waste time by worrying and being anxious, flip the switch on satan by making a decision to pray instead. Quote scriptures declaring God's promises to you, then decide to do something productive with your time.

Mental Torment

When you suffer from mental torment, satan has your mind bound and disturbed with constant reminders about past sins, hurts and regrets or even with imaginations of things that have not really occurred. The things that satan torments your mind with also affect your emotions causing you to feel angry, sad or fearful. If you have the same thoughts coming to your mind on a regular basis, you may be dealing with mental torment from the enemy.

There was a time in my life when satan attacked my mind with mental torment. I had been hurt in a relationship and even though I had decided and declared my forgiveness for the incident, in my mind I kept reliving the event. By continuing to drop thoughts of past hurt in my mind, satan was using them to keep me stuck in the past. Through fervent prayer and a declaration of God's Word, I was able to break free so my mind could be at peace.

If you are suffering from mental torment, the blood of Jesus can deliver you! God desires for your mind to be free of the past so you can have a peaceful mind and fully live out your purpose today. Know that God has already forgiven your past sins, so do not allow satan to condemn you any longer. Romans 8:1 says, "There is therefore now no condemnation to those who are in Christ Jesus, who do not walk according to the flesh, but according to the Spirit."

We need to let go of the past once and for all. Paul says it well in Philippians 3:13-14, "Brethren, I do not count myself to have apprehended; but one thing I do, forgetting those things which are behind and reaching forward to those things which are ahead, I press toward the goal for the prize of the upward call of God in Christ Jesus." We need to let go of the pains of the past before we can fully embrace God's prosperity.

Double-Mindedness

A person who is double-minded is a person who has difficulty making and sticking with decisions. Double-mindedness causes you to be constantly unsure of yourself and your ability to handle life. You vacillate between doing this activity or that activity. You're never really sure if you belong in this ministry department or another one. At times, your indecisiveness causes you to simply do nothing, because you feel in that instance you can't make the wrong decision. You walk around in a constant state of confusion and indecision. In all of this, you are missing God's best for your life.

James 1:5-8 says, "If any of you lacks wisdom, let him ask of God, who gives to all liberally and without reproach, and it will be given to him. But let him ask in faith, with no doubting, for he who doubts is like a wave of the sea driven and tossed by the wind. For let not that man suppose that he will receive anything from the Lord; he is a double-minded man, unstable in all his ways."

Being double-minded causes you to be unstable, undependable, lacking in commitment. Since stability, dependability and commitment are all necessary components to living a prosperous life, we have to get rid of double-mindedness.

Sometimes we become double-minded because we analyze things too much. Our intelligence and reasoning ability get the best of us. The Bible tells us to "Trust in the LORD with all your heart, and lean not on your own understanding; In all your ways acknowledge Him, and He shall direct your paths." (Proverbs 3:5-6) When it says we should not lean on our own understanding, it is referring to our reasoning and analytical ability. Don't trust your intelligence over the leading of the Holy Spirit. Learn to walk by faith in God and make decisions by depending on God.

Doubt and Unbelief

To have doubt means that you have a state of uncertainty in your life. You have belief in God's Word but you have not fully settled in your mind that you are trusting in the Word that you believe. When you have unbelief, you don't believe the Word. There are some people in the body of Christ who have picked and chosen what scriptures of the Word they will believe in. For instance, some say that the miracles and gifts of the Spirit like physical healing that we see operating in the book of Acts was only for the first century and are not for today. So because of their unbelief, they rarely see healings in their churches.

If you doubt that God's promises apply to you, then you will never see the fruit of those promises manifested in your life. Over and over in the gospels, Jesus told the person he was ministering to, "Be it unto to you *according to your faith.*" Know that God loves you personally and is intimately concerned about your life and purpose. All of his promises are for you as well as anyone else. Sometimes we feel that we are not worthy to receive God's best, that it is reserved for someone more important.

I love the story in the Bible about the woman with the issue of blood in Mark 5:21-43. Jesus was on his way to Jairus' house to heal his daughter when the woman with the issue of blood pressed through the crowd to touch Jesus' garment and get her healing. Jesus stopped what He was doing to find out who touched Him because He knew that the healing power had gone out of His body. When she came to Jesus, afraid and trembling, Jesus ministered to her kindly. He called her "daughter" a term of relationship and declared that her faith had made her "whole". I believe she was not only healed in her physical body but all the emotional issues of shame, hurt and rejection were healed as well.

It is interesting to me that when Mark recorded this story that he took much care to record Jairus' name and his title; he was a ruler in the synagogue. However, he did not feel it important to record the woman's name that had the issue of blood. During that era, women were not regarded as important in that culture. However, Jesus felt she was so important that He stopped what He was doing to minister to her needs.

You are equally important to God. Believe today that all of God's promises are for you to claim. Even though others may not acknowledge you, God knows your name and He is waiting for you. Cast off doubt and unbelief and begin today to fully believe His Word applies to you. Then Jesus will say to you as well, "Be it unto to you *according to your faith.*"

Tiredness

Too often in our society, we work more than we should and rest less than we should. Our physical bodies have limitations and when we ignore those limitations, we set ourselves up for an attack by the enemy. When we are physically tired, satan can use our lack of energy to attack the mind.

When God created the world, He did His work of creation in six days and then He rested on the seventh day. By doing so, He set a pattern for us to follow. Later with the Israelites, He commanded them to keep the Sabbath holy. They were not allowed to do any work on the Sabbath.

Although we are no longer under the law or bound to honor Saturday as the Sabbath, I believe God still wants us to set aside a day for rest each week. Taking time to rest will keep your body and your mind fresh and alert. It will also help you guard against the attacks that satan inevitably launches on those who are overly tired physically.

I have experienced satan's attack on my mind when I am tired. He tries to put all types of crazy thoughts in my mind. However, since I am aware of his tactics, I command those thoughts to go in Jesus' name. Then I go and take a nap! Take time to rest your physical body, it will help you in your quest to live a life of prosperity in every area.

Resentment and Bitterness

When you fail to forgive someone who has wronged you, it causes you to resent that person, or have unresolved anger towards him or her. I've heard resentment described as "frozen rage", which in essence means that your rage is frozen momentarily but with the right provocation, it will come gushing out. Resentment and a lack of forgiveness almost always lead to bitterness. The word, "bitter" means to have a sharp and unpleasant taste. A person with a bitter personality is sharp and unpleasant to deal with!

Satan uses the two darts of resentment and bitterness to make you feel you have a "right" to hold onto your anger because of the depth of the hurt that you suffered. Because you feel victimized, satan will remind you of your pain so you hold onto the resentment and bitterness as long as possible. The only problem with this attack is that it robs *you* of your joy and peace. The person who hurt you is probably not even thinking about the incident anymore, while your life is on hold because of your pain.

In Matthew chapter 18, it tells about a servant who owed the king a large sum of money, like $9.6 million. The king demanded payment, however, because the servant did not have the money he begged the king for an extension of time to pay. The king had compassion on him and *forgave* the entire debt.

The servant never quite heard and received the message that he was forgiven of the debt so he went to a fellow servant who owed him a small amount, about $16. When the fellow servant couldn't pay, he had him thrown into jail. When the king heard about it, he threw the first servant in jail where he was tormented.

The moral of the story is that we have to receive God's forgiveness for ourselves first because we have all missed the mark with God. Secondly, we need to extend the same grace and forgiveness to others that God has shown to us. When we don't forgive others, we end up in prison in our minds tormented by resentment and bitterness. These negative emotions drain our energy and cause us to miss God's best for our lives. Make a decision today to forgive and let go of the hurts so there will be nothing blocking God's prosperity from flowing in your life.

Getting Free from Satan's Attacks

If you have continual mental attacks from satan, you probably need to be delivered from the oppression he is causing you. Satan is a defeated foe because Jesus destroyed him when He died on the cross. "For this purpose the Son of God was manifested, that He might destroy the works of the devil." (I John 3:8) However, even though satan is defeated, he still walks around looking for someone to devour. He will attack you in the area of your weakness. When we say negative things and speak words of doubt, fear and unbelief, we give satan an entrance to attack our thoughts.

James 4:7 tells us, "Therefore submit to God. Resist the devil and he will flee from you." This verse gives us a two-step process for our deliverance. First, we need to submit ourselves to God. Having a right relationship with God is paramount for your living a peaceful, prosperous life. It starts with confessing Jesus as Lord and Savior, but it continues on a daily basis as we confess our sins, seek forgiveness and maintain our fellowship with the Father through prayer and Bible study.

Second, we need to resist the devil. The word "resist" means "to withstand, fend off, to oppose actively or to fight against," according to Webster's dictionary. Resisting is spiritual warfare. Our weapons are the Word of God, the blood of Jesus and the name of Jesus. Use all three on a regular basis to get and maintain your freedom from satan's attacks. Jesus is our example in Matthew 4 where He responded to every one of the enemy's attacks with a verse of scripture. We should do the same. In the chapter on "Developing a Prosperous Mind", we will use the scriptures to transform your mind.

There is a peace that God wants for His people, a place of rest and serenity that allows us to clearly hear the Holy Spirit as He speaks to us. Hebrews 4:9 says, "There remains therefore a rest for the people of God." When we are in that place of peace, our mind is at peace, our days become more productive, our lives become more meaningful, our jobs become more enjoyable and we begin to make giant strides towards reaching our destiny. In short, we are able to live a prosperous life in every respect.

Satan Attacks Your Mind

Don't allow satan to keep your mind bound any longer. Confess your faith in God with this prayer of deliverance. "Father God, I thank you that Jesus defeated satan at Calvary. I declare that 'greater is He that is in me than he that is in the world'. I am more than a conqueror through Christ Jesus. I submit myself afresh to you God, cleanse me of all unrighteousness and make me more like Christ. I renounce every mind-binding spirit that satan would try to put on me right now in the name of Jesus. I renounce every spirit of distraction, worry, anxiety, mental torment, double-mindedness, doubt, unbelief, tiredness, confusion, resentment, bitterness and any other attack of the enemy on my mind in Jesus name. I declare that I have the mind of Christ. The blood of Jesus covers my mind. Thank you, God, for renewing my mind, restoring my hope and blessing me with a productive and prosperous life. In Jesus Name, Amen."

Remember that changing your thinking patterns is a process not a one-time event. You will have to daily submit yourself to God, daily believe and confess His Word and daily resist satan so he will flee. Don't allow satan to steal your joy, your passion or your peace. Take control of your thought life today so you can be free. II Corinthians 10:4-5 says, "For the weapons of our warfare are not carnal but mighty in God for pulling down strongholds, casting down arguments and every high thing that exalts itself against the knowledge of God, bringing every thought into captivity to the obedience of Christ." Living a life of prosperity is a daily walk of victory over the enemy.

CHAPTER 5

TRANSFORMING YOUR MIND

We live in a society that has many issues and challenges. The economy is cyclical moving from times of economic boom to times of economic bust. We get excited when the economy is doing well then we fret when the economic outlook is bleak. When we turn on the news, we are bombarded with negative news of calamities, job layoffs, company closures, wars, hurricanes, floods, murders and unrest.

Looking at the negative state of the world can impact your mind and cause you to live life with a pessimistic view of things. In the midst of all the challenges that we face, how do we react? The world would have us fearful, worried and filled with anxiety. This is not God's plan for His people. God's people should never respond to life's challenges the same way that the world does. We are in the world but not of the world. Therefore, we need to have a different mindset than the world does in handling life's events.

The Bible lets us know how important our thoughts are. In Proverbs 23:7, it says, "As a man thinks in his heart, so is he." We become what we think about. In Romans 12:1-2, it says "I beseech you therefore, brethren, by the mercies of God, that ye present your bodies a living sacrifice, holy, acceptable unto God, which is your reasonable service. And be not conformed to this world: but be ye transformed by the renewing of your mind, that ye may prove what is that good, and acceptable, and perfect, will of God."

First, God wants us to give ourselves to Him completely. We present our bodies as a living sacrifice. This is really an oxymoron, because to make a sacrifice usually means that you kill whatever it is that you are sacrificing, but God asks us to present our bodies as a "living sacrifice". This is possible because we must crucify the flesh. Our fleshly desires must die.

The Word says that those who try to save their lives will lose their lives. But those who are willing to lose their lives for God's sake will find their lives. As we give up our desire to do what we want to do when we want to do it and say to God like Isaiah, "here I am Lord send me," then we become a living sacrifice. We have sacrificed our life, yet because we are still alive, we can accomplish God's purpose in the earth.

Verse two says we should not be "conformed to this world" but "transformed by the renewing of our mind". To conform means to become similar to, to be in agreement with, to act in the same way. In other words, we conform by acting just like the world does. When your boss at work is giving out pink slips and everyone is complaining around the water cooler, God's people shouldn't be joining in. After all, God is our source and not our employer. When we are thinking the same way as the world, we are conforming not transforming!

The Bible admonishes us to be transformed by the renewing of our minds. The word, "transformed" comes from Greek word, metamorphoo (met-am-or-fo'-o); which is where we get our word, metamorphosis. It means to change in form, structure, or function; like the physical change undergone by a caterpillar to a butterfly.

The word "renewing" speaks of a process. If it were "renew", it would speak of a one-time action. The "ing" means it is something you have to continually do;

every day. We practice renewing our minds by learning to think in ways that please the Lord. The Bible tells us that He will keep us in perfect peace if our minds are stayed on Him.

Thinking on the Word of God as opposed to the circumstances of life and items in the news media can greatly increase your peace of mind and allow you to live a life of victory and peace in the midst of difficult situations.

How can we change our mind? And more importantly, how can we change our circumstances? I believe that success is a process, which we can have great influence over. If we are to change our circumstances, it all starts with the thoughts in our minds.

The process of success is as follows:

Thoughts → Feelings → Words → Actions → Character → Destiny

Start At the End

The Bible says God has predestinated us. In Romans 8:29-30, its says, "For whom he did foreknow, he also did predestinate to be conformed to the image of his Son, that he might be the firstborn among many brethren. Moreover whom he did predestinate, them he also called: and whom he called, them he also justified: and whom he justified, them he also glorified."

The word, "predestinate" is an interesting word. It is the combination of two words, "pre" and "destination". The prefix "pre" means before in time, place and rank. The word "destination" means the place toward which one is going or sent; the purpose for which someone or something exists. When you put the two together, it means that our destiny was determined before.

God has a destiny for each one of us. He did not haphazardly create anyone. In fact, God determined your purpose before you were created. He told Jeremiah that before he was in his mother's womb, He had already sanctified him and ordained him as a prophet to the nations (Jeremiah 1:5).

Likewise, God has already determined your purpose in the earth. It is our job to first develop a relationship with God through faith in Jesus Christ so that we can restore communion and fellowship with the Father. Once we have the ability to communicate with God, it is our responsibility to discover our purpose, dwell on it in our thought life, develop our gifting and abilities, and then discipline ourselves to do the thing that God has called and purposed for us in the earth.

Habakkuk 2:2-4 says, "Then the LORD answered me and said: "Write the vision and make it plain on tablets, that he may run who reads it. For the vision is yet for an appointed time; but at the end it will speak, and it will not lie. Though it tarries, wait for it; because it will surely come, it will not tarry. Behold the proud, his soul is not upright in him; but the just shall live by his faith." (NKJ)

By spending time in prayer and consecration before God, He will reveal to you the purpose for your life. Write it down and then begin to prepare yourself for your destiny through study, training and service. With a God-directed purpose for your life, I believe it is possible to have true success and peace of mind. Once we have discovered our purpose, then we need to direct our thoughts towards our intended destination.

Our Thoughts Are Powerful

Our thoughts are the seeds that lead to our destiny. If we think correctly, it can cause us to live a life of faith and purpose propelling us to our destiny. However, if we think thoughts of doubt, fear and unbelief, it will paralyze our potential. Every device that has ever been invented started off as a thought in someone's mind. We can think about possibilities and progress. Or we can dwell on problems. The choice is up to us.

Have you ever noticed how you can think about a situation that happened five years ago and invoke all of the same emotions that you felt then? That is because your thoughts are powerful. If someone hurt you five years ago and you think about that incident right now, you will feel the same emotions of anger that you felt then. It's best to resolve that anger by forgiving the person so you can move on with your life.

Your thoughts lead to your feelings. When you think thoughts of faith, you feel more confident in the Lord. When you think thoughts of fear, you feel more doubtful. The solution is to change your thought life.

Paul knew the power of thoughts when he told us in II Corinthians 10:5 that we should "cast down imaginations, and every high thing that exalts itself against the knowledge of God, and bring into captivity every thought to the obedience of Christ." Our mind can imagine a lot of things that are against the things of God. The important thing is to first of all recognize what our dominant thoughts are and then replace the negative, sinful thoughts with Godly, purposeful thoughts.

You may be thinking that this is easier said that done. But actually, it's a matter of developing new habits. In this technologically advanced age in which we live, it is easy to write out a faith-filled confession that you can record and listen to twice a day until it changes your thinking pattern. You can also make it a habit to listen to Praise and Worship music in your car and home to set an atmosphere of God's presence throughout the day.

The Word of God tells us what to think about in Philippians 4:8, which says, "Finally, brethren, whatsoever things are true, whatsoever things are honest, whatsoever things are just, whatsoever things are pure, whatsoever things are lovely, whatsoever things are of good report; if there be any virtue, and if there be any praise, think on these things." (KJV) If what we are thinking about is not a good report, we need to focus on something else.

Here is a faith-filled confession that you can use in your life to begin to change your thoughts to what God's says about you.

> I am who God says I am. I am called, anointed and appointed by God. I am the head and not the tail. I am above and not beneath. Everything I do prospers. The favor of God is upon my life. I am fearfully and wonderfully made. I have been made in the image of God Almighty. I am the child of the King. God loves me unconditionally. I have been blessed with all spiritual blessings in heavenly places in Christ Jesus. I have been forgiven of all my sins. I have been redeemed. I am a peculiar person, unique in Christ Jesus. I am accepted in the Beloved. God has chosen me. God has endowed me with gifts. I walk in abundant life. I am a joint heir with Christ Jesus. All my needs are met by His riches in glory. I have the peace of God reigning in my life.

> The joy of the Lord is my strength. I am a winner of the race. I am the apple of His eye. My steps are ordered by God. I fulfill my destiny every day. To God be all the Glory!

Our Thoughts and Feelings Lead to Our Words

The things that we think about cause use to feel a certain way, which affects what we say and how we say it. Words are extremely important. In fact words have creative power. In Genesis 1, God spoke and created the world. He said over and over, "let there be" and it was so. By speaking a creative word, God brought forth the world, the land, the seas and oceans, day and night and all of creation. Hebrews 1:3 tells us that the whole world is being held together by the "Word of His power". God's power springs out of His Word.

We are made in the image and likeness of God. So the words we speak also have power. Our words can change the very course of our lives. Proverbs 18:21 says, "Death and life are in the power of the tongue: and they that love it shall eat the fruit thereof." So many times people speak death to their situation rather than life. People will say things like, "I am always broke," "I am always a day late and a dollar short," or "There is always so much month left at the end of my money." Then they wonder why they are always broke and in debt. They are speaking death to their finances.

We need to change what we say about our situation to agree with the truth of God's Word. How about saying things like, "I am blessed and highly favored of God," or "My God is supplying all of my needs according to His riches in glory by Christ Jesus," or "Jehovah Jireh is my provider." I am not suggesting that we deny reality or fail to deal with reality. I am suggesting, however, that we need to think on the things of God in order to build our faith while we are doing everything we know to do in the natural to handle the situation.

Just because the circumstances of life are not exactly as we want them to be does not mean that we have to be sad, discouraged or mad. In fact, our faith in God should shine even more greatly in difficult times. If it doesn't, then how are we any different than the world? Remember, we are to be transformers not conformers!

Our Words Cause Our Actions

The things that we do in life are a direct result of what we have been thinking about whether positive or negative. When we think thoughts of faith and purpose, we begin to take action based on the destiny we are trying to reach. On the contrary, when we think thoughts of doubt and fear, we become discouraged (or lose our courage), causing us to do nothing.

For example, before I wrote my first book, Stop Robbing Peter to Pay Paul, I wasted many years doing nothing on the project. The reason was because of what I was saying to myself in my thought life. I said things like, "I can't write a book and if I do, who is going to read it?" I told myself that God already had a lot of other qualified people writing on Biblical stewardship so I wondered why I needed to write another book on that subject.

But as I began to listen to the voice of God, He let me know His plan, which I allowed to change my thinking. What God revealed to me, I began to say to myself, "God has given me special insight into *why* people spend their money the way that they do. I have something important to say and God is going to give me the contents of this book and the audience that needs to read it." As I changed my thoughts on the matter, my actions changed and I began to set aside time to write the book. After the book was released, I began to receive countless testimonials from people attesting to the fact that it had changed their lives. It was a word that God needed to get into the earth and I had to be the obedient vessel to publish that word in a book. I give all the glory to God!

James 1:22 says "But be ye doers of the word, and not hearers only, deceiving your own selves." Our faith in God is not really faith until we take action on it. Whatever word God has given to you is your specific assignment in the earth. Stop procrastinating and start taking action by faith on what God has commissioned you to do. Put your faith to work by taking action on what God has spoken to your heart. God will bless your obedience to Him.

Our Actions Determine Our Character

Our character is what makes us unique. It speaks of our faith, our morals, our results whether good or bad, our integrity and reputation. Your actions determine your character. Faith-filled actions that change people's lives give you character as a spokesperson for God.

Our actions need to be different from the worlds. All my life, I have always been a little different. When I was younger and less mature, I was bothered by the fact that I never quite seemed to fit in with the crowd. I was always a loner in school, never part of the "in-crowd", with only a few friends. As I have matured in the Lord, I realized that I am supposed to be different. In fact, I found myself in the Bible when it said that I should be peculiar!

I Peter 2:9 says "But ye are a chosen generation, a royal priesthood, an holy nation, a *peculiar* people; that ye should show forth the praises of him who hath called you out of darkness into his marvelous light."

How we think and act needs to be rooted in the Word of God and not the world. When we do what's right according to God's Word in the midst of opposition, persecution and difficult times, it shows that we truly are Christians.

Our Character Leads to Our Destiny

When we are living, breathing, thinking and doing the will of God for our lives, we end up at the assigned destiny He has for us. God has a plan for each one of our lives. His plan for us is a place of peace, provision and purpose. When you are operating in the place of ministry and service to mankind that God has for your life, you will know it! There will be a "peace that passes all understanding". You will flow in your assignment - the struggle to prove who you are will be gone. You will know and know that you know that you are where God wants you to be.

Jeremiah 29:11 says, "For I know the plans I have for you, declares the Lord, plans to prosper you and not to harm you, plans to give you hope and a future." (NIV) It's important to remember that God's destiny for you has an "appointed time" according the Habakkuk 2:3. Sometimes we get into trouble by trying to rush God's timetable. We need to respect the process of growth and development needed before we can reach our destiny. If we rush to our destiny without proper preparation or at the wrong time, it can destroy us. However, when we go to our destiny at God's appointed time, we will be fully equipped to handle whatever situation that arises.

Facts and Truth are not the Same

Our place of destiny is similar to the Promised Land that God gave to the Israelites. It was a place that flowed with milk and honey and had grapes so large you needed two people to carry one cluster! I often wonder why I don't see grapes that large in my local supermarket.

When we look at the nation of Israel, God had given them a Word that declared that the Promised Land would be given to them as their inheritance forever. The Word that God declared was the truth, however, the circumstances presented some facts that were contrary to the truth of God's Word.

Numbers 13:26-33

26 Now they departed and came back to Moses and Aaron and all the congregation of the children of Israel in the Wilderness of Paran, at Kadesh; they brought back word to them and to all the congregation, and showed them the fruit of the land.

27 Then they told him, and said: "We went to the land where you sent us. It truly flows with milk and honey, and this is its fruit.

28 Nevertheless the people who dwell in the land are strong; the cities are fortified and very large; moreover we saw the descendants of Anak there.

29 The Amalekites dwell in the land of the South; the Hittites, the Jebusites, and the Amorites dwell in the mountains; and the Canaanites dwell by the sea and along the banks of the Jordan."

30 Then Caleb quieted the people before Moses, and said, "Let us go up at once and take possession, for we are well able to overcome it."

[31]But the men who had gone up with him said, "We are not able to go up against the people, for they are stronger than we."

[32]And they gave the children of Israel a bad report of the land which they had spied out, saying, "The land through which we have gone as spies is a land that devours its inhabitants, and all the people whom we saw in it are men of great stature.

[33]There we saw the giants (the descendants of Anak came from the giants); and we were like grasshoppers in our own sight, and so we were in their sight.

Numbers 14:24

[24]But My servant Caleb, because he has a different spirit in him and has followed Me fully, I will bring into the land where he went, and his descendants shall inherit it.

All of the 12 spies that went into the Promised Land to spy it out saw the same things, but their thoughts about the situation were different. It's not what happens to you in life that matters, it is how you look at it. The land was exactly as God had described it – filled with milk and honey, fruit, real estate and blessings. And yes, there were giants in the land as well. It was a fact, but not the truth.

The 10 spies who gave the congregation a negative report saw themselves as grasshoppers fighting giants. Joshua and Caleb, however, had their faith firmly rooted in God's Word. They saw their God fighting the giants for them, "Let's go, we are well able to do this!" They did not compare themselves to the size of the giants so that they were filled with fear as the 10 spies were. They compared the giants to the size of their God, causing their thoughts to be those of faith.

Numbers 14:24 tells us that Caleb had a different spirit. Do we? First, we need a personal relationship with God through faith in Jesus Christ. Then, we need to think on the truth of God's Word, not the facts of this world. The truth of God's Word is always more important that the facts of the situation.

It is easy to find application of this principle to our daily lives. The newspapers and television are always full of negative news. They may report that these are tough economic times. However, we can counter that fact with the truth of God's Word in Psalms 37:18-19, "The LORD knows the days of the upright, and their inheritance shall be forever. They shall not be ashamed in the evil time, and in the days of famine they shall be satisfied."

There may be reports of rising prices or a crash in the stock market. This may be the fact that the media is reporting, however, we can rest on God's Word that says, "But seek ye first the kingdom of God, and his righteousness; and all these things shall be added unto you." Matthew 6:33

You may have lost your job and the unemployment rate may be high, so the prospect of finding another job may be bleak. However, you don't need to focus your thoughts on these facts, but on the truth of God's Word. Psalms 37:25 says, "I have been young, and now am old; yet have I not seen the righteous forsaken, nor his seed begging bread." Psalms 5:12 says, "For You, O LORD, will bless the righteous; with favor you will surround him as with a shield." The favor of God means that when you are in fellowship with God, He will bless you with a new job even in a tough job market.

Change your thinking from the facts of the news media to the everlasting truth of God's Word. Make a faith confession based on the Word of God. Read it every day. Listen to praise and worship music. Don't allow the news media to set your atmosphere. Set your own atmosphere. You can transform your mind by meditating on the Word of God on a daily basis.

Chapter 6

Developing a Prosperous Mindset

What do you think and say to yourself about your financial situation on a daily basis? It is important because as I discussed in a previous chapter, your thoughts and words will determine your course in life and can bring death or life to your financial situation.

Developing a prosperous mindset is imperative to your financial success. But what exactly does the Bible teach on prosperity? The Bible tells us in III John 1:2, "Beloved, I pray that you may prosper in all things and be in health, just as your soul prospers." The word "prosper" in this verse comes from the Greek word, euodoo (yoo-od-o'-o), which means to do well on the journey or to succeed in reaching. It speaks of successfully reaching the destination God has purposed for your life.

This verse is profound because God wants us to prosper in every area of our lives, to walk in divine health and especially to have prosperity in our soul. The soul refers to the mind, will and emotions. We have to prosper in our mind, will and emotions *before* we will ever see the manifestation of prosperity in any other area of our lives.

The prosperity John is writing about here is not spiritual prosperity. He has already assumed and given a foundation that your soul should prosper. He has also already mentioned that we should walk in health. So I believe when he says here that he wants you to prosper, he's talking about financial means. We can now begin to see why there's confusion, even in the body of Christ, concerning materialism versus stewardship and prosperity versus poverty.

Jesus told us in John 10:10b, "I am come that they might have life, and that they might have it more abundantly." Abundant life is for here and now. It encompasses every area of your life, including your finances. A person who has achieved financial success, but has no peace of mind is the most miserable person of all.

Too often in the body of Christ, we are schizophrenic when it comes to money. On one end of the spectrum, you have those saints who believe that "poverty is next to godliness" so they renounce all earthly wealth and focus on spiritual things only. On the other end of the spectrum, you have those preaching a prosperity gospel that everyone in the body of Christ will be financially wealthy.

Some churches take up so many offerings that the people get offended and feel that the pastor is just after their money. Other churches don't emphasize giving at all so people don't feel it's important to give to church any significant amount.

Some pastors never preach on money so their people are left to figure out money matters on their own. While other pastors preach on money so much you'd think that's the only topic in the Bible. Congregants get the impression that the *only* way to prosperity is by giving to the church.

Some people proclaim that they teach a "prosperity gospel". Although God does desire to prosper His people, as we will see by the scriptures, prosperity should never be elevated to the level of a "gospel". The "gospel" or good news is salvation through faith in Jesus Christ as lord and savior period. Our mission as believers is to fulfill the great commission of bringing souls into the kingdom of

God. So the purpose of God's prosperity for us is to help us to accomplish His mission.

What is the answer? The truth needs to be found in the Word of God alone. We need to settle in our minds once and for all what God teaches in His Word about money, wealth and prosperity. Most importantly, we need balanced teaching on this subject that takes into account the whole counsel of God.

This chapter will focus on helping you to change your money mindset with the Word of God. It will bring balance to the issue of money using the scriptures to show how God wants to bless your life in all areas. The result of submitting to God's way of doing things is that He brings the prosperity to your life. The goal is to change your mindset to a prosperous one by the power of God's Word.

As you begin to think on God's Word, it builds your faith in the area of financial prosperity. You can then begin to speak the Word of God over your circumstances in faith. As we learned in a previous chapter, what we think about affects our feelings. Our thoughts and feelings lead to our actions. Our actions determine our character, which leads to our destiny. If your goal is to live a more prosperous life, then it starts with you changing your thoughts about money and prosperity to what God's Word says about it.

This chapter is organized like a daily devotional so that you can read one section per day and then meditate on the scripture that is referenced for that day. Research has shown that it takes 21 days to form a new habit, so this section covers 21 days of devotions. If you can discipline and focus your mind to concentrate on prosperity scriptures for 21 days, it can help you create a more prosperous life!

It may be helpful for you to memorize the scriptures that are highlighted. You may also want to start a journal to write your thoughts of how God is changing your thinking. Write down any ideas or strategies God may give you during your quiet times with Him and how your life is becoming more prosperous by implementing those ideas.

In the Appendix, there is a reference chart listing the 21 daily statements and scriptures along with another list of prosperity scriptures that you can meditate on for reinforcement of your new prosperous mindset.

Day 1 – I Daily Meditate on God's Word

"Blessed is the man who walks not in the counsel of the ungodly, nor stands in the path of sinners, nor sits in the seat of the scornful; but his delight is in the law of the LORD, and in His law he meditates day and night.
He shall be like a tree planted by the rivers of water, that brings forth its fruit in its season, whose leaf also shall not wither; and whatever he does shall prosper." Psalms 1:1-3

God's Word is incredibly powerful. It has the power to change your life, encourage you, strengthen you, and give you wisdom. There are so many promises of God in His Word that we are yet to enjoy because we have not fully grasped them. The only way to begin to enjoy all of the benefits of God's Word is by making it a habit to study and meditate on God's Word on a daily basis. At the end of this chapter, I give a list of prosperity scriptures. Use these scriptures as a starting point to meditate on God's Word and to change your thinking regarding God's desire to prosper you in all areas of your life.

I look at the Bible as my spiritual food. When I rise in the morning, I generally eat breakfast because my body needs nourishment. While eating breakfast, I read my Bible because my spirit needs nourishment also. Too often, believers only get their spiritual food when they go to church on Sunday. That is a mistake. What if you only ate physical food once a week? You would be malnourished, sick and would eventually die of starvation.

When we meditate on the Word of God, we are doing more than just reading it. We are taking time to think about it deeply, to reflect upon what is said, to envision how it applies to our lives. We take time to memorize scriptures that speak to our current situation. It becomes something that we think about during the day to keep us grounded in our lives.

When you meditate on the Word of God daily, you will prosper in every area of your life. The Word of God will not allow you to stay the same. As we read the Bible, it reads us! It acts as a mirror, reflecting the truth about ourselves to us. We see areas where we need to be delivered from strongholds, change behaviors, mend relationships, and obey God's commands. God is transforming us to be more like Jesus every time we read the Bible. II Corinthians 3:18 tells us, "But we all, with unveiled face, beholding as in a mirror the glory of the Lord, are being transformed into the same image from glory to glory, just as by the Spirit of the Lord."

When we discipline ourselves to meditate on God's Word both day and night, it will bring stability and peace to our lives. We will be rooted and grounded in the Word of God and know His promises for ourselves. Our confidence and faith in God will soar because the truth of God's Word makes you free.

Knowing God's Word and living out its principles is the key to living a life of prosperity in every area. This verse promises us that the result of meditating on God's Word is that we will be "like a tree planted by the rivers of water, that brings forth its fruit in its season, whose leaf also shall not wither; and whatever he does shall prosper."

The tree planted speaks of being rooted and grounded in the proper place of your destiny. Bringing forth fruit speaks of our productivity. We are utilizing our gifts and talents in a productive manner that is blessing other people's lives. Being in our season means that we are operating in the divine timing of God for our lives. "To every thing there is a season, and a time to every purpose under the heaven." (Ecclesiastes 3:1) And the end result of all of this is that it brings forth prosperity in everything that we do.

Day 2 – I Honor God First

"Honor the LORD with your possessions, and with the firstfruits of all your increase; so your barns will be filled with plenty, and your vats will overflow with new wine." Proverbs 3:9-10

What an awesome God we serve. When we truly see the magnitude of His greatness, power and majesty, we should stand in awe and reverence. It should prompt us to want to honor Him not for what He has done for us but simply for who He is.

When we honor someone, we show the highest regard and respect for that person. God is creator and sustainer of this universe. He is our provider, protector, peacemaker, refuge, savior, warrior, and so much more.

When we honor God with our money by giving to Him first, it demonstrates our faith and utter dependence on Him to provide for our needs. It shows that truly He is lord over our lives.

In the Old Testament, there was concept called first fruits. When God spared the lives of the firstborn of the Israelites as the death angel killed the firstborn of the Egyptians, God sanctified the firstborn of the Israelites as holy and sacred. The principle was extended to include the first fruits of the land. "In general, first fruits included those in the raw state (grain and fruit); those prepared for use as food (wine, oil, flour, and dough), including wool," according to the New Unger's Bible Dictionary.

The law did not give a lot of guidelines for the first fruits offering, according to Unger's. "The law nowhere specifies the amount that was to be given in the shape of offerings of this kind but leaves it to each individual's discretion; it only provided that the choicest portions were always to be offered."

In today's time, we do not harvest fruits and grains, we work at a job and earn a salary from which we can return the tithe and give an offering to the Lord. In keeping with the principle of first fruits, however, I believe you should write the first check to the Lord's work. Honor God before you pay your mortgage, car note and credit cards.

The Bible also says, "where your treasure is, there will your heart be also." As we honor God first with our treasure, it strengthens our faith in God. When we return the tithe, the first fruits of our salary, we redeem the other 90% of our money – we purchase it back from being under the curse. We bring our finances under the blessings of God. I don't know about you, but I would rather shop with 90% money that is blessed by God than to try to shop with 100% money that is under a curse.

When we write our check for the tithe and offerings first, we live out that Scripture which says, "the just shall live by faith." It takes faith to write a check to your church before you calculate whether you will have enough money left over to pay your other bills. But we believe in the same God who took one boy's fish sandwiches and fed over 5,000 people. If God can multiply fish and bread when it is dedicated to Him, surely He can multiply your monthly income to cover your bills.

Make a decision today to begin to live by faith and to honor God with the first fruits of your income. Begin to return the tithe to your local church where you are fed the Word of God and to give to other ministries as the Lord leads you. The concept of first fruits in the New Testament is symbolic of the abundant life that Jesus died for us to have. So as you faithfully, consistently honor God first with your income, He will prove His faithfulness to you and bless you to live an abundant and prosperous life.

Day 3 – I Live on Purpose

"Before I formed you in the womb I knew you; before you were born I sanctified you; I ordained you a prophet to the nations." Jeremiah 1:5

"For I know the plans I have for you," declares the LORD, "plans to prosper you and not to harm you, plans to give you hope and a future." Jeremiah 29:11

God has designed you for a specific purpose that only you can fulfill. When you have discovered your purpose and are operating in it, then God's financial resources will flow to you to allow you to fulfill your assignment. You also need to be in the right position to receive God's prosperity. The right position means being in the right place at the right time so the blessings of God can flow in your life.

We need to be careful in life that we don't settle for less than God's best for our lives. God had promised the Israelites real estate, a land flowing with milk and honey, pomegranates, grapes and blessings. To receive their blessing, they had to cross over the Jordan River and take possession of it. Two of the tribes of Israel, Reuben and Gad, didn't want to go. In Numbers chapter 32, they begged Moses to let them settle on the east side of the Jordan because they had cattle and too much stuff to cross the river. Basically, their material things were more important to them than obeying the voice of God so they settled for less than God's blessing for their lives.

Hundreds of years later, the descendants of the tribe of Gad encounter the powerful healing ministry of Jesus Christ in Mark chapter 5. Instead of receiving the long-anticipated Messiah, they tell Him to get out of town because their pigs got destroyed when Jesus cast the demons out of a man. The decision of their ancestors had become a generational curse for them because they too were more interested in their material possessions than obeying God.

What about you? Where does God want you to be? I urge you to prayerfully seek God's will for your life, family relationships, job, career, and education. Finding your purpose in life is your number one assignment. If you are not clear about your lifetime assignment, then take some time to spend in fasting and prayer to seek God's leading.

You can also utilize different assessment tools that will help to determine your spiritual gifts, skill sets and natural talents. These tools can provide helpful insight, but be aware than your skill set in the natural or your occupation may be a means for providing for your family, however, it may not be God's assignment for your life.

Another way to help discover your assignment is to ask yourself some questions. What do you love to do so much that you would do it even if you did not get paid? What are you passionate about? What problem in the world burdens you? Your role may be to solve that problem.

If God is telling you to launch into ministry, then that is where He will bless you. If God is telling you to start your own business, then do the research, get the experience, and go for it! If He is telling you to seek a promotion on your job, then apply for that next level of responsibility. Do what God is telling you to do and the blessings will follow! God will provide all the financial resources to meet your needs, your assignment and your ability to manage it. Whatever God is telling you to do, trust Him completely and go for it!

Day 4 – God Owns My Money

"For every beast of the forest is mine, and the cattle on a thousand hills. I know all the birds of the mountains, and the wild beasts of the field are mine. If I were hungry, I would not tell you; for the world is mine, and all its fullness."
Psalms 50:10-12

We need a big attitude change here. We tend to think, "I own my skills, knowledge and abilities. I go to work; I make this money so it's mines." That's the wrong attitude. Everything that we have belongs to God.

In the parable of the talents, the lord gave to the servants, "his goods". God gives us money to manage but He is the owner of the money. Some people get bent out of shape when ministers tell them to give ten percent of their income to God. Well, I'm a little radical on this subject. I tell people to give God 100% of their money. Give it all to God; it belongs to Him anyway.

This is about attitude and accountability. When we look at the money as belonging to God, it causes us to be accountable to Him for how we manage it. We want God to be pleased with what we have done with His resources.

In my book, Stop Robbing Peter to Pay Paul, I elaborate on this concept.

> Think of it like an owner of business. If I own a shoe store, for example, then I am in charge of all of operations of that facility. I put marketing plans in place to generate revenues and control expenses so that I can earn a profit. I can decide that out of the profits of my business I am going to give a gift to John. Would John have the right to ask to look at my financial records to see if I could have given him a larger gift? Of course not, he should just be grateful for the gift.
>
> Let's change this scenario a little. Now I am manager of a shoe store that John owns. He has delegated responsibility for day-to-day operations of the store to me. He has instructed me on the marketing plans to use to generate revenues and the expenses to control so that I generate a profit. Now I write a check to John. Does John have the right to ask to see the complete financial records of the business? Of course he does,

> he is the owner of the company and I work for him.
>
> God tells us in His Word that we are managers of His assets. We can go all the way back to Genesis to establish this fact. God created the heavens and the earth. Whenever someone creates something, they own it. In our society, people obtain patents, copyrights, or trademarks in order to protect the ownership of something that they have created. Since God created everything, He owns it.

There is a song that Frank Sinatra used to sing called, "I did it my way." That should never be the song of a believer. We were bought with a price, so everything that we own and all the resources that we have should be used to glorify God.

To establish God's ownership of your money, why not start praying about all financial decisions before you make them. Ask God what ministries you should donate to, what you should spend money on, what areas you need to cut back in, and what new ventures you should pursue. God is willing to guide us in the management of the resources He has entrusted to us. But first, we must be willing to ask for His assistance.

Day 5 – I Tithe to God Regularly

" 'Bring all the tithes into the storehouse, that there may be food in My house, and try Me now in this', says the LORD of hosts, 'If I will not open for you the windows of heaven and pour out for you such blessing that there will not be room enough to receive it. And I will rebuke the devourer for your sakes, so that he will not destroy the fruit of your ground, nor shall the vine fail to bear fruit for you in the field," says the LORD of hosts.' "
Malachi 3:10-11

Tithing represents ten percent of your gross income. But much more than a dollar amount, tithing regularly to God demonstrates your total faith in God over your money. It takes faith to write a check to your church for ten percent of your income before you calculate whether or not you will have enough to pay your other bills afterwards. It requires you to depend on God to supply all of your needs.

Some people get confused on tithing, thinking that because it is in the Old Testament, it is part of the Law and therefore, doesn't apply to the church since we are under grace. But tithing actually began over 400 years before the law was ever instituted. Abraham tithed ten percent of his spoils of war to his high priest, Melchizedek. His grandson, Jacob, also tithed prior to the law ever being instituted. Tithing was established as part of the everlasting covenant God established with Abraham. That covenant was a covenant of faith that we are now a part of as believers.

God asks His people to bring their tithes and offerings to His storehouse and to prove Him. He promises to open the windows of heaven and pour out a blessing so large that we cannot even contain it. The blessings that God pours out on us include ideas, strategies, favor, financial prosperity and protection.

God also promises to rebuke the devourer for our sakes so that we do not experience needless destruction and loss. Another way I like to look at it is this. When the Israelites were about to leave Egypt, the last plague that God released was the death of the firstborn. Through Moses, God instructed the Israelites to put the blood of a lamb on the doorposts of their homes. It demonstrated their faith in God. When the death angel came through, it saw the blood of the lamb and passed by that house. However, the Egyptian households did not have faith in God so they did not have any blood on their doorposts and the firstborn of their households died.

When we tithe faithfully to God, it is like putting blood on our doorposts. The death angel that seeks to devour our finances must pass by our house because our faith is in the living God to protect our finances and provide for all of our needs. I can tell you from experience as a faithful tither that God has protected our household from loss.

Tithing is so important to God that He considers it robbery if we fail to give ten percent of our income as a tithe. To spend the tithe is like stealing because it belongs to God. A failure to tithe brings a curse on our lives.

As we keep our covenant with God by tithing ten percent of our income, He is faithful to pour out His abundant blessings on us. But you can only tithe by faith. You can't start to tithe this week and then expect a check to arrive in the mail next week. God is looking for your faithfulness to tithe regularly. The only way you can tithe is to surrender control over your money to God. When you begin to tithe, you are saying to God that you are giving up doing it your way and you are willing to give Him the reins of your financial life. God is a dependable source.

Day 6 – I Work Hard

"And whatever you do, do it heartily, as to the Lord and not to men, knowing that from the Lord you will receive the reward of the inheritance; for you serve the Lord Christ." Colossians 3:23-24

"The hand of the diligent will rule, but the lazy man will be put to forced labor." Proverbs 12:24

Genesis chapters one and two give us God's original plan for mankind. Before the fall that brought sin into the world, God ordained work. When He created mankind, God gave Adam a job in the Garden of Eden. "Then the LORD God took the man and put him in the Garden of Eden to tend and keep it." (Genesis 2:15) Adam's job was to cultivate and maintain the garden, in other words, to work. This assignment was given prior to the fall of man. Contrary to what some people believe, work is not part of the punishment given to man after he sinned. After the fall, work became more difficult for man, but work was part of God's divine plan from the beginning.

In fact, work is one of the primary methods for us to obtain our financial resources. "Almost everyone in the Bible worked and worked hard. There were relatively few skilled occupations such as potters, metal smiths, masons, scribes, dyers, weavers, and jewelry makers. For the most part the life of the average person consisted of long hours of very hard work," according to Nelson's Illustrated Bible Dictionary. The Bible tells of many different occupations including armor bearers, bakers, bankers, builders, butlers, farmers, innkeepers and judges. The virtuous woman was a real estate investor. "She considers a field and buys it; from her profits she plants a vineyard." (Proverbs 31:16).

Although the Bible gives few details, Jesus was known throughout His hometown as a carpenter (Mark 6:3). Simon Peter ran a successful fishing business that received a supernatural increase in profits when Jesus told Peter exactly where to let his nets down at in order to catch a tremendous amount of fish (Luke 5:2-9). Jesus desires to lead us today in our business endeavors and show us profitable strategies as well. We just need to seek His guidance and wisdom as we make business decisions.

The Apostle Paul worked as a tentmaker along with Aquila and Priscilla. Tent making, a craft that was passed down from father to son, was an ancient craft that consisted of cutting and sewing together goat's haircloth, and attaching ropes and loops. Although Peter, Paul and even Jesus were awesome ministers of God, the Bible lists that they had jobs to provide for their financial needs. Likewise, we need to work a job.

As we work, God expects us to be diligent. To be diligent means to be hardworking, disciplined and committed to whatever task you are assigned. You persevere, you are persistent, and you don't give up easily in your quest for prosperity. You go above and beyond the basic requirements to give an excellent effort to your work.

So work hard on your job as unto the Lord. It may be a job in the secular arena, but work there with a spirit of excellence and faithfulness. To be faithful means you are reliable – you are there, consistently, day-in and day-out. Do what is expected of you; in fact go above and beyond. Be the light in darkness on your job. And God will bless your faithfulness to Him.

Enjoy your work; it is a gift from God. If you have a job that you enjoy, you are truly blessed. "I know that nothing is better for them than to rejoice, and to do good in their lives, and also that every man should eat and drink and enjoy the good of all his labor-- it is the gift of God." (Ecclesiastes 3:12-13)

Day 7 – I Have Prosperity for a Purpose

"And you shall remember the LORD your God, for it is He who gives you power to get wealth, that He may establish His covenant which He swore to your fathers, as it is this day." Deuteronomy 8:18

God gives us power to get wealth. Another word for "power" in this scripture is "ability". When we look at our knowledge, skills and abilities, we need to understand that all of these things came from God. He is the one who has equipped us to succeed in life.

When God allows financial prosperity to come to us, it is for a purpose. It is not for us to lavish ourselves with expensive stuff or to become materialistic. But the purpose of our wealth is so that God may establish His covenant in the earth.

I believe we are in the last days. Soon Jesus Christ will be descending with a shout with the voice of the archangel blowing the trumpet to rapture out the church of God. Before that happens, however, it is God's desire to bring the biggest harvest of souls into the kingdom that he possibly can. But he cannot do that without the help of the saints. When God prospers us financially, He wants us to give to ministries that are bringing souls into the kingdom.

I love the story of Rick Warren, founder and pastor of Saddleback Church in Lake Forest, California. According to a recent article in Reader's Digest, "Warren's first book – The Purpose Driven Church, published in 1995 and aimed at pastors – has sold a million copies. In 2002 he released The Purpose Driven Life, which has sold 30 million, making it one of the best-selling books of all time. He and his wife give away 90 percent of their income to charity, much of it anonymously; in 2004, the last year the figures were made public, they donated $13 million."

When God gave Warren the ideas to write those books, He already knew in advance how successful the books would become and how many lives would be helped by their messages. God also knew the heart of Warren. God knew He could trust him with all of that wealth. In response, Warren gives a lot of his wealth away to help spread the gospel message.

Just think about it, if you can give $50 a month to help a ministry spread the gospel to the world that would be great! But what if you could afford to give $500 a month? What about $5,000 a month? Think about how many more lives can be helped by the larger donations. The point is that the more God blesses you with, the more you can funnel into worthwhile ministries that can make a real difference in the world.

The fact of the matter is this – it costs money to operate ministries. Churches and para church organizations have to pay gas, electric and water bills just like you and I. And if a missionary wants to travel to a foreign country in order to spread the gospel, they have to pay for an airline ticket, meals and lodging as well. If a ministry wants to set up an orphanage to help homeless children, it requires the purchase of a building, hiring of staff, purchase of furniture and the whole nine yards.

If God blesses you to acquire wealth, then make sure your wealth has a purpose. Use a portion of your wealth to bless the lives of others and to help to spread the gospel message to the world. God admonishes us to give liberally so that the needs of others can be met. II Corinthians 8:15 says, "He who gathered much had nothing left over, and he who gathered little had no lack." One of the definitions of prosperity is the idea of "no lack". It is not a dollar amount, but the fact that all of your needs are met. Remember, to whom much is given, much is required.

Day 8 – I Know God Gets Excited When I Prosper

"Let them shout for joy and be glad, who favor my righteous cause; and let them say continually, 'Let the LORD be magnified, who has pleasure in the prosperity of His servant.'" Psalms 35:27

This verse says that we should be shouting and excited when we are in line with God's agenda. Dr. Leroy Thompson Sr. describes it well in Money Cometh! To the Body of Christ, "What is God's righteous cause? It's the covenant. It's evangelism. It's going out to preach the Gospel. It's supporting people who preach the Gospel. I'm not just talking about supporting the local church; I'm talking about supporting people who go to the mission field too."

God is our heavenly father who cares deeply for His children. Just like a natural parent gets excited when their children do well, God gets excited when we do well. He wants us to live out our purpose, walk in dominion and have the necessary resources to accomplish His will in the earth.

In fact, I believe that God was bragging on Job to satan when He asked him, "Have you considered my servant Job, that there is none like him on the earth, a blameless and upright man, one who fears God and shuns evil?" (Job 1:8) Job was an extremely prosperous man, both in material and spiritual things. He feared God and served God wholeheartedly with all of his substance.

I have two adult children. If you give me a chance, I will talk your ear off bragging about them. I can tell you countless stories of them growing up and how they made me proud. Now that they are becoming young adults, I see them maturing and beginning to walk in the purposes for their lives.

My son, Dante, completed his Bachelor of Science degree with honors in business management and is now working on his master's degree. He knows the Lord and is working hard towards his goal of becoming a screenwriter. My daughter, Tiffany, is a brilliant young lady who earned a full-tuition scholarship to start her undergraduate studies. She also knows the Lord, loves children and will one day make an awesome teacher.

Why do I brag on my children? Because that's what proud parents do! When your children are doing something worthwhile with their lives, you just want to share your excitement with somebody.

Well, God wants to look down on us and do the same thing. He wants to see us living a full and productive life, using our gifts and talents to serve others and bring Him glory. In the process, God will be excited to see us prospering in all areas of our lives.

God has pleasure in the prosperity of good people, not only of His family, the church in general, but of every particular servant in His family. He rejoices when we prosper in material things and when we prosper in spiritual matters. God doesn't delight when we have grief and problems in our lives. When God does allow us to prosper, we should acknowledge His blessing with thankfulness and praise by saying, "The Lord be magnified."

As our success in life brings us financial prosperity, we will want to use part of those resources to support the furtherance of the gospel because of our relationship with the Lord Jesus Christ. As we do so, God gets even more excited because our prosperity is helping to spread the gospel message. In the end, God's goal is to bring all the kingdoms of this world into His kingdom. He wants souls to be saved and lives changed. The prosperity that God blesses us with should help to accomplish that purpose.

Day 9 – I Serve Others with a Spirit of Excellence

"Yet it shall not be so among you; but whoever desires to become great among you, let him be your servant. And whoever desires to be first among you, let him be your slave." Matthew 20:26-27

One of the wrong mindsets about money that we in the body of Christ need to change is thinking that money should just come to us and we don't have to *do* anything to get it, we just deserve it! In the church, we get confused on this issue.

The faith movement got some of us confused; we think all we need to do is confess the scriptures, believe God and our wealth is just going to show up in our mailboxes. We use catchy phrases like: name it and claim it, believe it and receive it, confess it and possess it, and blab it and grab it!

When the Israelites were in the wilderness, God dropped manna and quail from heaven to feed them. That was a special situation for the nation of Israel. Let me give a news flash - God is no longer dropping manna and quail from heaven! Even for the Israelites, once they got to the Promised Land, they had to fight for everything they got.

The expectation that we can get money by confession alone is why some of us are still broke. We are confessing it but we aren't doing anything. That is a wrong attitude; it really is a welfare, give me a handout mentality. God expects you to work. He ordained work before the fall. Before sin entered the world, God gave Adam a job, to tend and keep the garden. Work is God's will for your life; it is not part of the curse.

Jesus said in the scripture above that if you want to be the greatest, serve others.

Zig Ziglar says, "You can have everything in life you want if you will help enough other people get what they want." I believe that. Discovering a need in society, developing a cost efficient and effective way to meet that need, and serving your product or service in a spirit of excellence can create financial prosperity. People pay for excellent service.

We need to change our money mindset in this area. Don't seek money; seek to glorify God by serving others. What product or service can you offer that will meet the needs of others and bring you financial prosperity as well? When you discover something that you can be passionate about while serving others, it can be your ticket to financial prosperity.

Sometimes people will invite me to a meeting, saying, "Come to this meeting and you can make a lot of money!" I'm never interested, why? I am not interested in *just* making money. I want to do what I am passionate about, what I feel can truly benefit others and have a lot of money be the byproduct of me serving others with passion and purpose. There's a book called Do What You Love and the Money will Follow. I've never read the book but the title alone was all that I needed to help me realize that a purposeful life is about a lot more than just making money.

We see how excellent customer service brings prosperity in the example of two brothers, Dick and Maurice. Recognizing that society was becoming faster paced with little time for cooking, they started a restaurant in California and created the Speedy Service System. They set up their kitchen as an assembly line and focused their staff on filling each order within 30 seconds or less. Their concept became a tremendous success, brought them prosperity and made the restaurant, McDonalds a household name. The McDonalds brothers earned their wealth by meeting the needs of people. The same can hold true for you – the more people you can serve with a spirit of excellence, the greater your wealth will be!

Day 10 – I am a Generous Person

"One man gives freely, yet gains even more; another withholds unduly, but comes to poverty. A generous man will prosper; he who refreshes others will himself be refreshed." Proverbs 11:24-25

This verse gives a dynamic promise from God. It says that when we are generous in giving, we will gain even more. Those who are willing to give to meet the needs of others become more prosperous. God sees your heart and your actions of generosity and He prospers you because of it.

The opposite is also true. Stingy people end up broke. When you try to hold onto everything, selfishly looking out for yourself only and never willing to give to help someone else's situation, you end up in poverty.

The abundant life is not living from paycheck to paycheck barely making ends meet. The abundant life is living in the overflow, having enough financial resources to not only meet your needs but having excess so you can bless someone else, give generously to your church and other worthwhile ministries and make a difference in the lives of the people that you meet.

Generosity is an admirable trait. When you are generous, you have a heart that enjoys giving to others. To be generous means that you are willing to give and share, you are not selfish. God likes that type of attitude. I've heard it said, "What God can get through you, He can get to you." We are instruments of God. When He blesses us with resources, it is not always for our own use.

If you study the lives of wealthy people, more times than not, you will find that they are some of the most generous people. They will set up foundations for the sole purpose of giving away their wealth to worthy causes. In doing so, they become wealthier.

Bill Gates, one of the wealthiest men in the world, stepped down from running Microsoft, the company he founded, in order to spend the rest of his life giving away the majority of his wealth through the Bill and Melinda Gates Foundation. Through their generosity, they are making a dramatic impact on the world in the areas of science, technology, education and health care.

Their generosity has not gone unnoticed. Warren Buffett, the world's richest billionaire, announced that he would bequeath the bulk of his approximately $44 billion fortune to the Bill and Melinda Gates Foundation. The Gates' generosity brought them even more prosperity to manage!

As servants of the Lord, we are to be like a pipe. When you go to the bathroom to wash your hands, you cut on the faucet and expect water to flow. You don't think about the pipes in the wall and how they are connected throughout the house to the water meter, outside the home and underground all the way back to city water supply.

A pipe is a tube for conveying water, a conduit, or vessel. When you go to the bathroom, you're not looking for pipes but for water. Likewise, we are to be like pipes – a vessel that God can use to meet the needs of others. As the water flows through the pipes, the pipes themselves get wet, cleaned and refreshed by the water. Likewise, as God blesses us financially, our needs are met but the excess can flow through us to meet the needs of someone else.

So be generous, give freely, and share what you have with others. In doing so, God will honor your generosity and bless you with even more resources to manage.

Day 11 – I am Disciplined

"For God has not given us a spirit of fear, but of power and of love and of a sound mind." (NKJ)

"For God did not give us a spirit of timidity, but a spirit of power, of love and of self-discipline." (NIV)
II Timothy 1:7

I listed the same verse in two different versions above because by reading it in different versions, you gain a fuller understanding of God's intention. Sometimes we allow fear to keep us from being all that God has purposed for our lives. That fear causes us to be timid, shy or hesitant in pursuing God's best for our lives. We are holding back, not giving it our all, wasting time and making excuses.

The spirit of fear, which includes timidity, the tendency to hesitate, and that paralyzing sense of dread that causes you to do nothing comes from satan. He wants you to live your life beneath your potential. He wants you to settle for less than God's best for your life. He wants fear to rob you of fully living out the abundant life that Jesus died for you to enjoy.

By the power of the blood of Jesus Christ and the name of Jesus, we can renounce the spirit of fear and timidity and accept the spirit of power, love and self-discipline that God has given to us. When we operate in a spirit of self-discipline, it causes us to prosper.

It's been said that successful people are willing to do on a regular basis what unsuccessful people are not. Success leaves clues. One key component of living a prosperous life is that you must learn to discipline yourself. Discipline simply means "doing what you need to do, when you need to do it, whether you feel like it or not."

We can talk ourselves out of doing things. In a previous chapter, we talked about how satan attacks our minds with thoughts that bring confusion, doubt, fear and double-mindedness. When we are double-minded, it is as if our mind is split between two opinions. You cannot focus and work hard on your assignment if you are double-minded.

Webster's defines discipline as "training that develops self-control and efficiency." Its root comes from the same word as disciple, which is a "follower of any teacher or school." We are disciples of Jesus Christ so to become disciplined means that we have fully surrendered our will to the Lord Jesus and have learned how to tap into the power of the Holy Spirit within us to help us daily live a victorious and prosperous life. We have the power within us to live a disciplined, productive, prosperous life.

We have to gain control over our daily habits in order to be successful. Stephen Covey in The 7 Habits of Highly Effective People, says, "Habits are powerful factors in our lives. Because they are consistent, often unconscious patterns, they constantly, daily, express our character and produce our effectiveness … or ineffectiveness. …Habits have tremendous gravity pull – more than most people realize or would admit. Breaking deeply imbedded habitual tendencies such as procrastination, impatience, criticalness, or selfishness that violate basic principles of human effectiveness involves more than a little willpower and a few minor changes in our lives. …Once we break out of the gravity pull, our freedom takes on a whole new dimension."

God says He has given us a "sound mind", which means that we can focus on the things of God, His purpose for ours lives and discipline ourselves to do what God has called each of us to do on a daily basis. We can be disciplined in our thinking, our daily habits and all of our actions.

Day 12 – I Manage God's Resources Well

"For which of you, intending to build a tower, does not sit down first and count the cost, whether he has enough to finish it." Luke 14:28

"He also said to His disciples: "There was a certain rich man who had a steward, and an accusation was brought to him that this man was wasting his goods. So he called him and said to him, 'What is this I hear about you? Give an account of your stewardship, for you can no longer be steward.'" Luke 16:1-2

Because God is the owner of our money, we are accountable to Him for what we do with it. We need to effectively manage our money in a way that God would be pleased. Setting up a written budget is a good starting point. Every time I do a workshop on budgeting, I ask the audience how many have a written budget. It is usually less that 10 percent of the people in attendance. Most people do not have a written budget. Some people have an idea in their head of what bills need to be paid; others just let the money flow through their fingers with no idea of where it is going. They just know that at the end of the month, it is all gone.

A budget is simply a tool to help you plan the use of your finances. It lists your income and expenses and helps you determine which bills you will pay from each pay period. It is a plan to help you reach your financial goals. A budget will help you to live within your means and provide for your future.

In the scripture above, a rich man had a steward (or manager) whom he had entrusted with the responsibility of managing his wealth. The word had come back to him that this steward was wasting his money. The rich man was furious; he wanted a full accounting of everything the steward had done because he was about to fire him! Fortunately, the steward began to focus his energies on getting debtors to pay back the rich man so that he was able to keep his job.

We need to take an inventory of how we have managed the money that God has allowed us to be steward over. The first step is to do a spending inventory over a 30-day period. A spending inventory lists everything that you purchase whether by check, cash or charge. It helps you to know where your money is going. Then you can ask yourself the question, is this where I want the money to go? It helps you to identify areas of waste in your budget so you can make better decisions about the use of your money.

After you have done a spending inventory, begin to set financial goals and to write a budget designed to help you reach those goals. Your financial goals can be both short-term (getting out of debt, buying or remodeling a house, or going on vacation) and long-term (children's college education or retirement). When you set up your budget, remember to put your tithes and offerings first, then list all your other expenses.

How you manage the money God entrusts to you is important. God says, "He who is faithful in what is least is faithful also in much; and he who is unjust in what is least is unjust also in much. Therefore if you have not been faithful in the unrighteous mammon, who will commit to your trust the true riches?" (Luke 16:10-11) I believe that the true riches are the anointing and power of God. If you cannot handle money, how can you handle God's assignment for you life?

If you need help with your budgeting, please consult my first book, Stop Robbing Peter to Pay Paul (available online at www.StopRobbingPeter.com). In it you will find Spending Inventory, Budgeting and Get Out of Debt forms that you can use. The parable of the talents teaches us that when you are faithful and profitable managing the money God has given to you, you will be blessed with more to manage. So decide today that you will begin to use a written budget to help you better manage God's resources.

Day 13 – I Pay All My Bills on Time

"The wicked borrows and does not repay, but the righteous shows mercy and gives." Psalms 37:21

God sees everything that we do, which means that we need to strive to live an excellent life in every area. With regard to finances, some people miss this point. They borrow money, whether it is from a financial institution or from a friend or family member, and they don't pay it back. But in the next breath, they are asking God to bless their finances. It's not going to work.

As Christians, we have been made righteous by the blood of Jesus Christ. He took on our sins and gave us his righteousness. We thank God for our new position in Christ. Because we are righteous, we need to live like it. The scripture above says that when we don't pay back money that we have borrowed, we are acting like the wicked because righteous people give back what is owed.

I remember a time when I was counseling a client whom I'll call Marsha (not her real name) for a mortgage loan. When I looked at Marsha's credit report, I noticed several unpaid collection accounts, charge-offs and judgments listed. When I asked Marsha about these items, she got indignant. With much irritation in her voice, she snapped, "I don't know why those things are still on my credit report. Shouldn't they have fallen off after seven years?" I had to gently remind Marsha that if she owed the bills, she should pay them and if they were incorrect she should dispute them with the credit bureaus.

But her attitude is what caught my attention. She really had no intention or desire to pay those old bills. She just wanted them to go away. Marsha was a licensed associate minister at a local church. She could praise God and proclaim His Word on Sunday with exuberance, yet she saw no correlation between her Christian faith and her attitude about not paying her bills.

We love to quote parts of Deuteronomy 28. We say we are blessed in the city, blessed in the field, blessed when we come and when we go. We are the head and not the tail, above only and never beneath. Deuteronomy 28:1-2 gives the conditions of God's covenant for financial blessings. There is one small, but key word that should not be overlooked.

"Now it shall come to pass, *if* you diligently obey the voice of the LORD your God, to observe carefully all His commandments which I command you today, that the LORD your God will set you high above all nations of the earth. And all these blessings shall come upon you and overtake you, because you obey the voice of the LORD your God." Deuteronomy 28:1-2

The word "if" in these verses means that these blessings are conditional. In order to claim and participate in the blessings of verses 3-14 of this chapter, you must first fulfill the requirements. The conditions are to diligently obey the voice of God and to carefully observe and obey His commandments.

Sometimes it takes the greatest amount of effort to right the wrongs of the past. It is quite a humbling experience. But it can also cause a tremendous amount of growth in your life. If there are bills that you have neglected and refused to pay, go back and pay them. Make it right with your creditors so there will be nothing to hinder God's blessings from flowing in your life today.

Day 14 – I Walk in Love

"No one has seen God at any time. If we love one another, God abides in us, and His love has been perfected in us." I John 4:12

You may be wondering why walking in love would be an important component for living a prosperous life. People who hold onto grudges, offenses, anger and unforgiveness are not only some of the most unpleasant people to be around, they also have set up strongholds in their lives that will block the flow of blessings. So in order to live a truly prosperous life, you need to let some things go and walk in love.

The book of I John has the phrase "love one another" in it five times (I John 3:11, 3:23, 4:7, 4:11 and 4:12). The commandment to love others is so strong that John asserts that our love for others is the proof that we have truly been born again. When we show love to others, it shows that the love of God is dwelling in us. We should be compelled to love others as we reflect on the magnitude of God's love for us when we were living in sin. Since God is a spirit that no one can see, He depends on us to show the love of God to a sinful and dying world so that they can see God through us.

Loving a sinner may seem like an easy task because you can understand that sin has blinded that person's eyes. However, one of the biggest problems I see in the church today as a minister of the gospel is people who have been hurt in the church who are still carrying a grudge. We need to understand the role of the enemy in this endeavor.

Beware of the spirit of offense. Satan loves to get people off their assignment. In fact, once you are saved, his number one mission in your life is to make you ineffective as a Christian. One way he does this is through the spirit of offense.

The spirit of offense works like this – someone says or does something that offends you; or they don't say something or do something that offends you. How do you respond? As a Christian, we should respond with forgiveness, but too often we get offended and either avoid the person who offended us or leave that church and go to another one without resolving the issue.

There is a couple that I know whom I'll call Beverly and Jacob. Beverly had found her giftedness and was serving with the ministry to the homeless. You could tell she was in her calling because as she spoke of her role in the ministry, she was glowing. Her husband, Jacob, was serving in another areas of the church. An issue came up and the pastor had to bring correction to the husband. Instead of him receiving the correction, he got mad, took his family and left the church. Two years later, I ran into the wife at a store; they were still looking for a church home. I call this the "wandering in the wilderness" church transition. They had not found a place to settle because they had allowed a spirit of offense to rule them and cause them to leave the church to begin with.

The only way to continually walk in love is that you must be willing to forgive. Sometimes people in the church have more issues than anywhere else. But the Bible says the world will know we are God's disciples by our love for one another. If someone says something that offends you, forgive and walk in love. Forgiveness is a decision not to hold offenses against another person. It does not excuse a wrong but you decide that the person does not owe you anything because of the wrong. You give up your desire for revenge or retaliation and allow God to heal your hurts. Forgiveness blesses you because you are no longer in bondage to resentment, anger, hurt, and blame. You are free to fully live your life in the prosperity and abundance that God has for you.

"Love suffers long and is kind; love does not envy; love does not parade itself, is not puffed up; does not behave rudely, does not seek its own, is not provoked, thinks no evil; does not rejoice in iniquity, but rejoices in the truth; bears all things, believes all things, hopes all things, endures all things." (I Corinthians 13:4-7) Love covers over a multitude of sins. Love also forgives and forgets.

Day 15 – I Dream Big and Ask Big

"Now to Him who is able to do exceedingly abundantly above all that we ask or think, according to the power that works in us, to Him be glory in the church by Christ Jesus to all generations, forever and ever." Ephesians 3:20-21

"Ask, and it will be given to you; seek, and you will find; knock, and it will be opened to you." Matthew 7:7

Our God is an awesome God. He is all powerful and all knowing. Moreover, He is committed to giving us everything that we need to live a victorious life. One of the main reasons why so many believers live beneath their life of prosperity is because they have never fully tapped into all of who God is. I believe God wants us to dream big, and ask big requests of Him in faith believing that He will do it.

A lot of limitations that we have are limits in our own mind. Oftentimes, we have been limited by our upbringing. We learn from our parents, teachers, siblings and relatives what we can expect from life. If we had a positive environment to grow up in where we were encouraged to shoot for the stars, then great. But too often, our environment growing up was not that supportive. You may have been told negative things like, "you will never amount to anything," or "you are just like your father." Teachers can at times label students as being "slow" or "remedial" and that label can limit a person's life. Thank God, that we can renounce all of these negative labels from others and get our identity from Christ and through His Word.

We may have been limited financially growing up as well. If we grew up in a household where there was lack, debt and financial stress, we often repeat those same issues in our adulthood. Well, it is time to shake off all of the issues of the past.

I love the story of Jabez in the Bible. It's really only two verses, but it gives us powerful lessons on how not to allow the limitations of the past to determine our future. "Now Jabez was more honorable than his brothers, and his mother called his name Jabez, saying, 'Because I bore him in pain.' And Jabez called on the God of Israel saying, 'Oh, that You would bless me indeed, and enlarge my territory, that Your hand would be with me, and that You would keep me from evil, that I may not cause pain!'

So God granted him what he requested." (I Chronicles 4:9-10)

The Bible says that his mother called him Jabez because she had borne him in pain. His name means sorrow, a burden or miserable. Can you imagine what a hard time Jabez must have had when he was a boy? In his day, people were very focused on the meaning of names and his name meant misery. He probably was made fun of because of his name. You know how cruel children can be. But thanks be to God, we are not bound by our upbringing or trapped by former circumstances. We can rise from the ashes to think big and ask big so we can accomplish more for Him!

Jabez prayed for four key things. He prayed for grace, growth, guidance and godliness. Jabez asked God to bless him, that's God's grace for our lives. God tells us that His grace is sufficient for us to handle whatever situation we encounter. Second, Jabez prayed for growth by asking God to enlarge his territory. He was not satisfied to remain the same. He was interested in growth and expansion. He believed big and he asked a big request. Third, Jabez asked for God's hand to be upon him; he knew he needed God's guidance as he moved from his familiar territory to a new arena. Finally, Jabez prayed for godliness, that God would keep him from evil. He knew that living a prosperous life started with godly living. And the Bible says God granted his request. The lesson is clear – we have not because we ask not. So, begin today to dream big and ask big requests of God!

Day 16 – I Serve God and Use Money

"He who loves silver will not be satisfied with silver; nor he who loves abundance, with increase. This also is vanity." Ecclesiastes 5:10

"No one can serve two masters; for either he will hate the one and love the other, or else he will be loyal to the one and despise the other. You cannot serve God and mammon." Matthew 6:24

"But those who desire to be rich fall into temptation and a snare, and into many foolish and harmful lusts which drown men in destruction and perdition. For the love of money is a root of all kinds of evil, for which some have strayed from the faith in their greediness, and pierced themselves through with many sorrows."
I Timothy 6:9-10

The Bible speaks more about money than it does faith and prayer. I believe God put so many verses in the Bible about money because He knew that we would have challenges in this area. Although money is an important tool to have in life, it can never be elevated to the point of idolatry in your life. God let us know that there are two masters in this world – it's not God and satan – it's God and money! Satan knows most people are not going to become satan worshippers but if he can get you obsessed with money, then he's got you nonetheless.

We are warned in many scriptures about the dangers of a love for money. When obtaining money becomes your focus over and above God, then the money has a place of idolatry in your life. We have to be careful in this area.

Many people have lied, cheated, stolen, killed and covered up crimes for the love of money.

Money is a tool that can be used to accomplish a lot of things. In and of itself, money is neither good nor evil. It takes on the morals of the person who holds the money. As believers, when we are blessed with more money, we can provide for our households, live debt free and give more to the furtherance of the gospel. We use money as a tool to accomplish good things, but we serve God alone.

When people allow money to become their god, they are never satisfied. They become obsessed with materialism, expensive toys and stuff. No matter how much money they have or how many things they possess, they always want more. That is because they are trying to fill the deep void within them with material things. Only God can fill that void.

God tells us again in Luke 12:15, "Watch out! Be on your guard against all kinds of greed; a man's life does not consist in the abundance of his possessions." Worldly riches cannot buy peace of mind or salvation; neither can it buy the person out of the wrath of God that is coming upon the world.

We have to be careful as we seek to live a prosperous life that we are operating in God's divine will for our lives. We have to pursue ministry opportunities, business ventures and jobs because God is leading us to do them, not because of how much money we can make. Money cannot be our focus or our motive. But I do believe that when we are lined up with the will of God for our lives, He will bring the financial prosperity to us.

When God blesses us financially, there is peace. Proverbs 10:22 says, "The blessing of the LORD brings wealth, and he adds no trouble to it." Let God lead you to the divine place of your prosperity; let Him heal and deliver you in every area of your life; then when He bless you financially, you will have peace and joy.

Day 17 – I Manage My Time Well

"To everything there is a season, a time for every purpose under heaven."
Ecclesiastes 3:1

Time is the most precious resource that God gives us. It is the very fabric that makes up our life. God gives everyone the same amount of time – 24 hours in a day. But what we do with our time can be vastly different. A big component of creating a prosperous life is being able to effectively manage your time. When you manage your time well, you live a life of purpose, accomplish more, and feel good about your life.

The enemy knows it takes time to be successful in life so he will attack your time. When you sit down to work on your God-given assignment, that becomes the exact moment when you will be bombarded with distractions – your child starts calling your name, your mind starts to wander, the phone rings, or you notice a chore that needs to be done around the house. I heard it said that as believers we don't need to be concerned about weapons of mass destruction, we really need to be concerned about the enemy's weapons of mass distraction!

When you waste your time, you are really wasting your life. According to Nielson Media Research, the average person spends about four and one half hours a day watching television. While there's nothing wrong with watching an occasional show that you like on television, you have to be really careful not to just allow television to waste your time. If you didn't spend four and one half hours a day watching television, what else could you do with that time?

In order to effectively manage your time, you have to first have a clear vision for your life and goals that you are trying to accomplish. Based on your goals, you can list what activities are required to help you reach those goals. Then on a daily basis, you decide what activities to do with your time and assign a priority to each activity. Interruptions and distractions need to be managed in order for you to stay focused on the tasks for the day.

God has also given seasons to our life. The season of your life dictates what assignment you are to be working on at that time. For instance, when it is your season to flow in ministry, God aligns all of the resources for you to do that. He also gives you the anointing and grace to do the work of the ministry. You will have wisdom for operating in that assignment that can only be described as heaven-sent. We need to always be sensitive to the leading of the Holy Spirit so that we will know our season. To go forward in your purpose before your divine timing can bring destruction; to go forward in your purpose after your timing can cause you to miss your season all together.

Too often people miss it when it comes to knowing the season of their life. They may have received the call of God to go into ministry and then feel compelled to jump into ministry right then. The apostle Paul gives us an example of how to handle a call of God on your life. After his dramatic conversion experience on the road to Damascus, he felt a call of God to take the gospel message to the Gentiles. However, he did not immediately go into ministry. Instead he spent 17 years in Arabia and Syria in a time of consecration and communion with God to prepare for his ministry assignment.

Once you have a clear vision from God of your assignment, make sure you then spend the appropriate amount of time preparing for that assignment. Preparation can include formal or informal education, serving under someone who can mentor you, or serving in other roles before God places you in your ministry assignment.

In my own life, I have felt the call on God on my life to teach the gospel every since I was a teenager. However, God had me spend many years preparing for my ministry assignment. When my children were young, at times I was frustrated that I was not a minister at a church. Then the Lord let me know that my children were my ministry assignment during that season of my life.

Day 18 – I Bless the Poor

"He who has pity on the poor lends to the LORD, and He will pay back what he has given." Proverbs 19:17

Sometimes we forget the heart of God. He has a heart that is compassionate towards the poor and downtrodden people of society. His love for them is no less than His love for you and I. But the only way that God can minister to the needs of the poor is if we have the same compassion for them that God has and use our resources to help them.

When the Israelites harvested their crops, God told them not to go over their fields a second time to gather every bit of grain but to leave some for the gleaners. Gleaners were the poor people who came and got what was left in the fields after the harvest.

Likewise, we need to have some money left over to give to those people who are less fortunate. When I give offerings, I remember to set some money aside to give to the homeless shelters. The homeless shelters provide for people who have lost everything – their homes, jobs, money and family support. These people have no choice but to seek the help of a shelter or sleep on the streets.

The shelters that I support not only give homeless people a place to sleep and a meal to eat, but they also share with them the gospel of Jesus Christ so that their lives can be changed and their hope for life restored.

God says that when we give to the poor, it is like lending to the Lord. Poor people can never repay you for your generosity. But God sees your compassion and He will repay your kindness.

We do have to exercise caution, however, when it comes to giving to the poor. Often in most large cities, you will see people standing on the streets with a sign that says, "Will Work for Food" or "Please Help Me". It's difficult to know whether these people are legitimately in need or not. Of course, you always want to be led by the Holy Spirit in all that you do.

On one occasion, I was in Columbus, Ohio at a conference. A friend and I were about to walk into a fast-food restaurant for lunch when a man who looked like he was homeless and destitute approached us. He said he was hungry and asked me for money. I told him that I would not give him money, but since we were right outside of a fast-food restaurant, I offered to buy him a meal. While he was eating, I had the opportunity to share the gospel with him.

Jesus was concerned with the poor. He told the rich young ruler who came to Him at night to ask how to obtain eternal life that he should sell all that he had and give it to the poor. On several occasions, Jesus said that the gospel was to be preached to the poor. While at a feast at the home of a Pharisee, Jesus admonished the crowd to not just invite their friends and those with wealth or influence to their dinners, but to invite the poor so they would be blessed of God. If you invite your friends, you expect them to repay you in some way. But the poor cannot repay you.

It is clear from scripture that God is concerned about the poor and disenfranchised in society. We should be concerned also and do what we can to help the poor. If we can't give money to homeless shelters, we can give our time and serve meals in a shelter. Or give them clothes that are in good condition that we no longer need. We can also volunteer out time to teach at the shelters to help them see the goodness of God and how God desires to restore their lives.

Day 19 – I Walk in God's Favor

"A good man obtains favor from the LORD." Proverbs 12:2a

"For You, O LORD, will bless the righteous; with favor You will surround him as with a shield." Psalms 5:12

"For whoever finds me finds life, and obtains favor from the LORD." Proverbs 8:35

As believers, we truly are blessed and highly favored of God. Throughout scriptures, God has always sought a people who will honor Him as Lord of their lives and in response He would show Himself strong on their behalf. Because we have a covenant relationship with God, we have His favor. Webster's defines favor as, "friendly regard, approval, partiality, support and advocate". That means that as God's chosen elect, we have special privileges and preferential treatment over unbelievers.

"Favor can break through any barriers set before you, and it is available to every child of God," according to Kate McVeigh in The Favor Factor. "When you believe and activate your faith for God's favor, it will work for you. Someone may not particularly like you or your personality, but that doesn't matter. You're believing in God's ability to influence them, and His favor on your life is supernatural. In other words it supersedes natural circumstances."

Growing up, I was my mother's favorite child much to the chagrin of my two sisters. My mother made no apologies; she simply let everyone know that I was her favorite child. As her favored child, I felt I had a special place in my mother's heart; she protected me, encouraged me, gave me nice things, and would even cook special dishes that she knew I liked. My mother was my biggest cheerleader. I like to say that she was the founder and president of my fan club!

God looks at you in the same special way. He has a special place in His heart just for you. You are the apple of His eye. He is in your corner, protecting you, cheering you on, opening doors for you, giving you favor with people that you need for your assignment and even giving you special surprises that only God can give! God's favor is unconditional; you don't deserve it and certainly cannot earn it. But you do need to have faith and believe that God's favor is yours.

Because we are God's favored people, we have special privileges, benefits that we can enjoy based on our relationship with God. Psalms 103:2-5 says, "Bless the LORD, O my soul, and forget not all His benefits: Who forgives all your iniquities, who heals all your diseases,

Who redeems your life from destruction, who crowns you with loving kindness and tender mercies, Who satisfies your mouth with good things, so that your youth is renewed like the eagle's."

Whenever you start a new job, one of the first questions is "what kind of benefit package is available?" When we come into the kingdom of God, we can ask the same question. The Word provides us with the answer. We have access to awesome benefits from God. He has promised to be our protector, provider, loving heavenly father, friend, companion, advocate, and source of wisdom. In addition, He gives us love, joy, peace, security, hope and blessings too numerous to count. We can ask for wisdom and know that He will give it to us so we can live the abundant life (James 1:5). He hears and answers our prayers and has promised to give us everything we ask for if it lines up with His will for our lives (I John 5:14-15). Walk in God's favor for your life today!

Day 20 – I am Honest in Business Deals

"He who walks with integrity walks securely, but he who perverts his ways will become known." Proverbs 10:9

"The blessing of the LORD makes one rich, and He adds no sorrow with it." Proverbs 10:22

"A good name is rather to be chosen than great riches, and loving favor rather than silver and gold."
Proverbs 22:1

"Better is the poor who walks in his integrity than one perverse in his ways, though he be rich." Proverbs 28:6

God is always interested in our heart issues and our motives, not just the results of what we do. When we look at creating a more prosperous life, it's vitally important that we maintain our integrity in the process. Integrity means wholeness, completeness, soundness and honesty. The word "integrity" comes from the same root as the word "integer" which means a whole number as opposed to a fraction. In other words, a person of integrity has consistency within their personality – what they believe and what they say and what they do are all the same. A person lacking in integrity has a fractured personality – they believe and say one thing but do something different.

As you work to create financial prosperity for your household, be honest in all of your business deals. Take the high road and not the low road. Make integrity the foundation of your life's work. Do what you say you are going to do when you say you're going to do it. Lying and deceiving to gain wealth may be profitable in the short term, but it's deadly in the long term!

Occasionally, you will read in the paper about a well-known corporate executive who is being charged with misusing corporate funds in order to increase his own personal wealth. Then they spend millions of dollars on high-priced attorneys to try to defend themselves against the charges. In the end, they end up losing everything – their job, their wealth and their freedom as they are carted off to jail. So what did their dishonest gain really accomplish? Not much. They had a few years of lavish living and status but once their scheme was found out, they spent the rest of their lives paying for it. Plus their reputation was permanently destroyed in the process. Whatever good they accomplished in their careers was forever tainted in the media by their lapse in integrity.

When I worked in the mortgage industry, there were times I was offered dishonest opportunities. On one occasion I met with a woman who wanted to sell her rental property to the tenant. She told me that the tenant was not working. I told her it would be difficult for the tenant to qualify for a mortgage loan without a source of income. She suggested that I could just create some pay stubs and W-2s on the computer to present to the lender. When I told her that idea would be dishonest, she said she knew of other mortgage brokers who did it all the time to get loans approved. I suggested she go work with one of those brokers. I had made a decision to do honest mortgage deals and the lure of increasing my income was not enough for me to compromise my integrity.

Make a decision to live a life of honesty and integrity even when no one is looking but God. You will live with greater peace of mind. Plus, you will have the added benefit of being able to fully enjoy whatever prosperity your business venture provides because you know in your heart that you got it honestly. Allow God to take your business to the next level. When He blesses you financially, there is no sorrow, only blessings!

Day 21 – I am Out of Debt

"The rich rules over the poor, and the borrower is servant to the lender." Proverbs 22:7

"Owe no one anything except to love one another, for he who loves another has fulfilled the law." Romans 13:8

When we are in debt, we are in bondage. Jesus died to set us free from bondage. But we willingly become the slaves of lenders by borrowing money to finance our desired lifestyle. The use of credit cards to finance the purchase of clothing, entertainment, vacations and other material things can be a deadly trap. Although there are times when borrowing money is necessary in order to fund a major purchase such as a home or a car, you should always have a plan in place before the purchase for paying the debt off as quickly as possible.

If you don't think that being in debt is the same as slavery, then think for a moment on the current amount of bills that you owe. What do those bills require you to do? Pay them, of course. In order to pay your bills, you have to keep a job and use a substantial portion of your income to pay back your creditors.

If your current job does not pay enough, then you will feel compelled to try to work overtime, do projects on the side or take on a part-time job in order to be able to fulfill your obligations. Why? Because your lender rules over you. Deuteronomy 28 even says that when you are in debt, you are no longer the head, but you are now the tail because the lender is the head over you.

Your head, the lender, can even force you to pay your debt if you refuse to pay it voluntarily. He can have you summoned into court, have a judge rule that you owe the money, and then garnishee your paycheck or bank account in order to get the money that you owe. The lender can put a lien on your home, seize your personal belongings and sell them at an auction or take whatever lawful means necessary in order to get his debt paid by you.

In the Old Testament, God gave many instructions to the nation of Israel regarding debts between the tribes. They could not charge interest to their family only to strangers and they had to set up a repayment schedule that ensured that the debt would be repaid by the year of jubilee.

The year of jubilee was a year when all debts were paid off or cancelled so the entire nation was completely debt-free. They had a big celebration to commemorate the occasion. If everyone in our nation were completely debt-free, we would celebrate also!

We may not be able to get the entire nation debt-free, but we can certainly work on our individual households. Why not set a goal to get out of debt? Set up a plan of action, follow it and then when you reach your goal, have a celebration with your family! Set your first priority to pay off all credit card debt and personal loans. Next, target to pay off your car loans and student loans. The final debt to target is to pay off your mortgage loans.

Being debt-free gives you freedom and peace of mind. Now the decisions you make don't have to be based upon making sure certain debts are paid. Now you can make decisions based upon purpose and passion. Finally, you reach a place where you can set your financial goals in place and begin to learn how to make your money work hard for you rather you always having to work hard for the money. You can be generous in your giving and make a difference in the lives of others. That is how truly prosperous people think and act.

Conclusion

If you want a change, you will have to make a change. The definition of insanity is "doing the same thing over and over and expecting different results". The poverty mindset has gotten you to where you are today. If you want the abundance of prosperity in your life, it will start with a change in your mindset.

The prosperity mindset is not an excuse to quit your job or to expect wealth to begin pouring out of the sky. Be realistic. You have to become more disciplined in managing your money by setting up a budget, assessing where you are right now and paying your bills on time. More importantly, you need to honor God first with your tithes and offerings so that the blessing of God will be on your finances.

By focusing on changing your mindset from poverty to prosperity, you activate your faith that allows you to see greater opportunities for your life. You may decide to seek a promotion on your job, start your own business or launch out into ministry.

Whatever you do, just understand that prosperity is a lifestyle not a get-rich-quick formula. You can't plant a seed and expect a full-blown rose bush the next day. Likewise, as you change your money mindset and begin working on your financial future, it will take time to see the progress.

Set your first goal to change your thinking and to increase your faith for financial prosperity. Then set financial goals for where you want to be a year from now, three years from now and five years from now. Believe that God desires for you to live the abundant life and walk in the prosperity he has provided for you. Make prosperity a lifestyle of making continual progress towards your God-given purpose. Then God will provide the abundant resources for you to be successful. To God be all the glory!

CHAPTER 7

ETERNAL PROSPERITY

Financial challenges are stressful enough without having to go through them alone. Although this book has provided strategies to change both your attitude and actions regarding money, its Bible-based principles will be more effective if you have a relationship with the Lord Jesus Christ. The principles in this last short chapter are the most important of all and should be the first step in your journey towards financial victory.

Each one of us is born with a void deep within us. Many people spend a lifetime trying to satisfy that deep longing of the heart. We may try to fill that void with material things, money, education, career, status or relationships but ultimately none of those things will provide lasting fulfillment. Only Jesus Christ can fill that void within you.

If there has never been a time in your life when you have given your life to Jesus Christ, now is the time to do so. You may be a member of a church, however, God is not looking for a religious ritual; He is looking for a personal relationship. God has a specific plan for your life, but He can only speak to you and guide you if you have a relationship with Him.

Wherever you are right now, you need to recognize that you need God in your life. The Bible says in Romans 3:23, "For all have sinned, and come short of the glory of God." We have all made mistakes in our lives. But God has made a way for us to be in fellowship with Him. John 3:16 says, "For God so loved the world, that he gave his only begotten Son, that whosoever believeth in him should not perish, but have everlasting life."

To be saved, you just need to confess your faith in Jesus Christ through prayer. Romans 10:9-10 says, "That if thou shalt confess with thy mouth the Lord Jesus, and shalt believe in thine heart that God hath raised him from the dead, thou shalt be saved. For with the heart man believeth unto righteousness; and with the mouth confession is made unto salvation."

If you want to receive Jesus Christ as your Lord and Savior, then please pray the following prayer in faith.

> Dear God, I admit to you that I am a sinner and that I need you. Please forgive me for all the sins of my life. I believe that Jesus Christ is the Son of God and that He died on the cross for my sins and rose again on the third day. I receive you now Jesus as my Lord and Savior. I believe in my heart and I confess with my mouth that Jesus is Lord. Thank you God for saving me. By faith in your Word, I am now born again! In Jesus Name, Amen.

If you have prayed the above prayer in faith, you are now born again. Welcome to the family of God! Your next step after salvation is that you need to join a Bible-teaching church where your faith can be strengthened and you can grow in your relationship with God. Allow the Holy Spirit who now lives inside of you to teach you and guide you in everything you do.

Appendix

Chart: 21-Days to a More Prosperous Life

Day 1 – I Daily Meditate on God's Word

"Blessed is the man who walks not in the counsel of the ungodly, nor stands in the path of sinners, nor sits in the seat of the scornful; but his delight is in the law of the LORD, and in His law he meditates day and night.
He shall be like a tree planted by the rivers of water, that brings forth its fruit in its season, whose leaf also shall not wither; and whatever he does shall prosper." Psalms 1:1-3

Day 2 – I Honor God First

"Honor the LORD with your possessions, and with the firstfruits of all your increase; so your barns will be filled with plenty, and your vats will overflow with new wine." Proverbs 3:9-10

Day 3 – I Live on Purpose

"Before I formed you in the womb I knew you; before you were born I sanctified you; I ordained you a prophet to the nations." Jeremiah 1:5

"For I know the plans I have for you," declares the LORD, "plans to prosper you and not to harm you, plans to give you hope and a future." Jeremiah 29:11

Day 4 – God Owns My Money

"For every beast of the forest is mine, and the cattle on a thousand hills. I know all the birds of the mountains, and the wild beasts of the field are mine. If I were hungry, I

would not tell you; for the world is mine, and all its fullness."
Psalms 50:10-12

Day 5 – I Tithe to God Regularly

"'Bring all the tithes into the storehouse, that there may be food in My house, and try Me now in this', says the LORD of hosts, 'If I will not open for you the windows of heaven and pour out for you such blessing that there will not be room enough to receive it. And I will rebuke the devourer for your sakes, so that he will not destroy the fruit of your ground, nor shall the vine fail to bear fruit for you in the field," says the LORD of hosts.'"
Malachi 3:10-11

Day 6 – I Work Hard

"And whatever you do, do it heartily, as to the Lord and not to men, knowing that from the Lord you will receive the reward of the inheritance; for you serve the Lord Christ."
Colossians 3:23-24

"The hand of the diligent will rule, but the lazy man will be put to forced labor." Proverbs 12:24

Day 7 – My Prosperity has a Purpose

"And you shall remember the LORD your God, for it is He who gives you power to get wealth, that He may establish His covenant which He swore to your fathers, as it is this day." Deuteronomy 8:18

Day 8 – I Know God Gets Excited When I Prosper

"Let them shout for joy and be glad, who favor my righteous cause; and let them say continually, 'Let the LORD be magnified, who has pleasure in the prosperity of His servant.'" Psalms 35:27

Day 9 – I Serve Others with a Spirit of Excellence

"Yet it shall not be so among you; but whoever desires to become great among you, let him be your servant. And whoever desires to be first among you, let him be your slave." Matthew 20:26-27

Day 10 – I am a Generous Person

"One man gives freely, yet gains even more; another withholds unduly, but comes to poverty. A generous man will prosper; he who refreshes others will himself be refreshed." Proverbs 11:24-25

Day 11 – I am Disciplined

"For God has not given us a spirit of fear, but of power and of love and of a sound mind." (NKJ)

"For God did not give us a spirit of timidity, but a spirit of power, of love and of self-discipline." (NIV)
II Timothy 1:7

Day 12 – I Manage God's Resources Well

"For which of you, intending to build a tower, does not sit down first and count the cost, whether he has enough to finish it." Luke 14:28

"He also said to His disciples: "There was a certain rich man who had a steward, and an accusation was brought to him that this man was wasting his goods. So he called him and said to him, 'What is this I hear about you? Give an account of your stewardship, for you can no longer be steward.'" Luke 16:1-2

Day 13 – I Pay All My Bills on Time

"The wicked borrows and does not repay, but the righteous shows mercy and gives." Psalms 37:21

Day 14 – I Walk in Love

"No one has seen God at any time. If we love one another, God abides in us, and His love has been perfected in us." I John 4:12

Day 15 – I Dream Big and Ask Big

"Now to Him who is able to do exceedingly abundantly above all that we ask or think, according to the power that works in us, to Him be glory in the church by Christ Jesus to all generations, forever and ever." Ephesians 3:20-21

"Ask, and it will be given to you; seek, and you will find; knock, and it will be opened to you." Matthew 7:7

Day 16 – I Serve God and Use Money

"He who loves silver will not be satisfied with silver; nor he who loves abundance, with increase. This also is vanity." Ecclesiastes 5:10

"No one can serve two masters; for either he will hate the one and love the other, or else he will be loyal to the one and despise the other. You cannot serve God and mammon." Matthew 6:24

"But those who desire to be rich fall into temptation and a snare, and into many foolish and harmful lusts which drown men in destruction and perdition. For the love of money is a root of all kinds of evil, for which some have strayed from the faith in their greediness, and pierced themselves through with many sorrows."
I Timothy 6:9-10

Day 17 – I Manage My Time Well

"To everything there is a season, a time for every purpose under heaven." Ecclesiastes 3:1

Day 18 – I Bless the Poor

"He who has pity on the poor lends to the LORD, and He will pay back what he has given." Proverbs 19:17

Day 19 – I Walk in God's Favor

"A good man obtains favor from the LORD."
Proverbs 12:2a

"For You, O LORD, will bless the righteous; with favor You will surround him as with a shield." Psalms 5:12

"For whoever finds me finds life, and obtains favor from the LORD." Proverbs 8:35

Day 20 – I am Honest in Business Deals

"He who walks with integrity walks securely, but he who perverts his ways will become known." Proverbs 10:9
"The blessing of the LORD makes one rich, and He adds no sorrow with it." Proverbs 10:22

"A good name is rather to be chosen than great riches, and loving favor rather than silver and gold." Proverbs 22:1

"Better is the poor who walks in his integrity than one perverse in his ways, though he be rich." Proverbs 28:6

Day 21 – I am Out of Debt

"The rich rules over the poor, and the borrower is servant to the lender." Proverbs 22:7

"Owe no one anything except to love one another, for he who loves another has fulfilled the law." Romans 13:8

Prosperity Scriptures to Meditate On

"The LORD will command the blessing on you in your storehouses and in all to which you set your hand, and He will bless you in the land which the LORD your God is giving you." Deuteronomy 28:8

"For You, O God, have tested us; you have refined us as silver is refined. You brought us into the net; you laid affliction on our backs. You have caused men to ride over our heads; we went through fire and through water; but You brought us out to rich fulfillment." Psalms 66:10-12

"This Book of the Law shall not depart from your mouth, but you shall meditate in it day and night, that you may observe to do according to all that is written in it. For then you will make your way prosperous, and then you will have good success." Joshua 1:8

"But seek first the kingdom of God and His righteousness, and all these things shall be added to you." Matthew 6:33

"Give, and it will be given to you: good measure, pressed down, shaken together, and running over will be put into your bosom. For with the same measure that you use, it will be measured back to you." Luke 6:38

"But this I say: He who sows sparingly will also reap sparingly, and he who sows bountifully will also reap bountifully. So let each one give as he purposes in his heart, not grudgingly or of necessity; for God loves a cheerful giver. And God is able to make all grace abound toward you, that you, always having all sufficiency in all things, may have an abundance for every good work." II Corinthians 9:6-8

"Happy is the man who finds wisdom, and the man who gains understanding; For her proceeds are better than the profits of silver, and her gain than fine gold. She is more precious than rubies, and all the things you may desire cannot compare with her. Length of days is in her right hand, in her left hand riches and honor." Proverbs 3:13-16

"I love those who love me, and those who seek me diligently will find me. Riches and honor are with me, enduring riches and righteousness." Proverbs 8:17-18

"He who has a slack hand becomes poor, but the hand of the diligent makes rich." Proverbs 10:4

"The rich man's wealth is his strong city; the destruction of the poor is their poverty." Proverbs 10:15

"The blessing of the LORD makes one rich, and He adds no sorrow with it."
Proverbs 10:22

"Riches do not profit in the day of wrath, but righteousness delivers from death." Proverbs 11:4

"He who trusts in his riches will fall, but the righteous will flourish like foliage." Proverbs 11:28

"There is one who makes himself rich, yet has nothing; and one who makes himself poor, yet has great riches." Proverbs 13:7

Appendix

"A good man leaves an inheritance to his children's children, but the wealth of the sinner is stored up for the righteous." Proverbs 13:22

"He who loves pleasure will be a poor man; he who loves wine and oil will not be rich."
Proverbs 21:17

"By humility and the fear of the LORD are riches and honor and life." Proverbs 22:4

"The rich rules over the poor, and the borrower is servant to the lender." Proverbs 22:7

"He who oppresses the poor to increase his riches, and he who gives to the rich, will surely come to poverty." Proverbs 22:16

"Do not overwork to be rich; because of your own understanding, cease!" Proverbs 23:4

"A faithful man will abound with blessings, but he who hastens to be rich will not go unpunished." Proverbs 28:20

"One who increases his possessions by usury and extortion gathers it for him who will pity the poor." Proverbs 28:8

BIBLIOGRAPHY

Avanzini, John. Financial Excellence: A Treasury of Wisdom and Inspiration. Harrison House, Tulsa, OK, 1993.

Brown, Kenneth. LIFE: Living in Freedom Everyday, Ken Brown International, Walled Lake, MI, 2008.

Cannon, Carl M. "Rick Warren: Man on a Mission", Reader's Digest, February 2009.

Cerullo, Morris. How to Prosper in the Current Financial Crisis, Morris Cerullo World Evangelism, San Diego, CA, 2008.

Chatzky, Jean. Talking Money: Everything You Need to Know about Your Finances and Your Future, Warner Books, New York, NY, 2001.

Covey, Stephen. The 7 Habits of Highly Effective People, Simon and Schuster, New York, NY, 1989.

Danker, William. Profit for the Lord: Economic Activities in Moravian Missions and the Basel Mission Trading Company, Wipf and Stock Publishers, Eugene, OR, 1971.

Eberle, Harold R. Developing a Prosperous Soul, Volume 1: How to Overcome a Poverty Mind-set, Worldcast Publishing, Yakima, WA, 1997.

Eberle, Harold R. Developing a Prosperous Soul, Volume 2: How to Move into God's Financial Blessings, Winepress Publishing, Yakima, WA,1997.

Eker, T. Harv. Secrets of the Millionaire Mind: Mastering the Inner Game of Wealth, Harper Collins Publishers, New York, NY, 2005.

Godwin, Rick. Training for Reigning, Charisma House, 1997

Hinn, Benny. The Gift: The Miracle of Unexpected Abundance, Bookmark Publishing, Dallas, TX, 2008.

Bibliography

Holy Bible, New King James Version.

Joyner, Rick. Overcoming the Spirit of Poverty, Morning Star Publications, Fort Mill, SC, 1996.

Love, Vicky Spring. Stop Robbing Peter to Pay Paul: The ABCs to Financial Victory, Victory Jubilee Publishing, Southfield, MI, 2003.

Maxwell, John C. The 21 Irrefutable Laws of Leadership: Follow Them and People Will Follow You, Thomas Nelson Publishers, Nashville, TN, 1998

McVeigh, Kate. The Favor Factor: Releasing God's Supernatural Influence to Work for You, Harrison House, Tulsa, OK, 1997.

Meyer, Joyce. Battlefield of the Mind: Winning the Battle in Your Mind, Warner Faith, New York, NY, 1995.

Miller, Darrow L. and Guthrie, Stan. Discipling Nations: The Power of Truth to Transform Cultures, YWAM Publishing, Seattle, WA, 2001.

Murdock, Mike. 31 Reasons People Do Not Receive Their Financial Harvest, Wisdom International, Denton, TX, 1997.

Nelson's Illustrated Bible Dictionary. Thomas Nelson Publishers, 1986.

Sauder, Brian. Prosperity with a Purpose, House to House Publications, Ephrata, PA, 2003.

Thompson Sr., Dr. Leroy. Money Cometh! To the Body of Christ, Ever Increasing Word Ministries, Darrow, LA, 1996.

About the Author

Dr. Vicky Spring Love

God has anointed Dr. Vicky Spring Love as a powerful teacher of the Word, bringing change and wholeness to everyone she ministers to. Although she teaches on all aspects of Christianity, she has a particular anointing in the area of financial victory and is passionate about helping people get their finances in order so that their money can bring glory to God. She has ministered in the area of financial victory for over 25 years as a conference speaker, workshop leader and writer.

Dr. Vicky's first book, Stop Robbing Peter to Pay Paul, is a powerful book that challenges people to be delivered from the real issues that cause their money problems. The book covers both the supernatural blessings of God and the natural responsibilities of the believer, including budgeting, getting out of debt, and cleaning up your credit. Stop Robbing Peter to Pay Paul was selected as the textbook for the Finances and Stewardship class at Destiny School of Ministry, which has 34 locations worldwide. This book, Changing Your Money Mindset, will also be used as a textbook at the school.

Dr. Vicky co-authored another book, 101 Great Ways to Improve Your Life, along with Jack Canfield (Chicken Soup for the Soul), John Gray (Men are from Mars, Women are from Venus), and Richard Carlson (Don't Sweat the Small Stuff). In addition, she has developed several other powerful, life-changing teaching CDs. Writing is a big part of God's ministry for Dr. Vicky. Her writings have appeared on www.streamingfaith.com, an online Christian television network featuring programming and editorials by other Christian ministers including Joyce Meyer, Bishop Eddie Long, and Dr. Myles Munroe. She has also been featured in The Detroit Free Press and on several television shows including "Live with Glenn Plummer" on CTN, "Detroit Alive" and "Public Report" on TCT, and "The Alabaster Box".

Dr. Vicky is a licensed minister of the gospel and an associate minister at Family Victory Fellowship (FVF) in Southfield, Michigan under the leadership of Pastors Larry and Sylvia Jordan. At FVF, she is dean of the Ambassador Bible Training School, a two-year bible school affiliated with FVF.

An entrepreneur at heart, Dr. Vicky has owned several business ventures including a real estate investment firm, a residential mortgage company and a communications company. She earned a doctorate of Religious Education degree from Destiny Christian University, a Master of Business Administration degree in Finance from Oakland University and a Bachelor of Arts degree in Communications from the University of Detroit.

Although Dr. Vicky serves in many capacities, she feels her first ministry is at home. She and her husband, Glen, have enjoyed a wonderful marriage since 1981, and are the proud parents of two adult children.

Other Resources from Dr. Vicky Spring Love

Stop Robbing Peter to Pay Paul
The book that is changing lives worldwide! Unlike any other book on money management, it helps you to discover what motivates you to spend money the way that you do. It teaches both the spiritual and the practical, including forms to set up a budget, a plan of action for getting out of debt, and steps to improve your credit.
160 pages **$18.00**

101 Great Ways to Improve Your Life - This dynamic book shows you how to achieve success in every area of your life – reaching goals, creating wealth, getting out of debt, and maintaining positive relationships.
Co-authored with Jack Canfield (Chicken Soup for the Soul), John Gray (Men are from Mars, Women are from Venus), Richard Carlson (Don't Sweat the Small Stuff) and others.
396 pages **$20.00**

Other Resources from Dr. Vicky Spring Love

Taking Authority Over Your Finances CD – Break every generational curse that is affecting your finances including a spirit of debt, lack, ignorance and settling for less than God's best for your life in this powerful, yet humorous, teaching! **$10.00**

Financial Crisis: The Cause & Our Response, 2 CD Set - With keen insight as a 15-year veteran of the mortgage industry, Vicky clearly explains what caused this crisis, how our nation has plunged from being under the blessing of God to being under a curse, and key strategies you can implement now. **$15.00**

Healing for Damaged Emotions CD – Emotional hurts from the past may be still affecting you today, even causing physical illnesses. But Jesus Christ knows how you feel and is able to heal you emotionally. Be delivered today through the powerful anointing of the Spirit. **$10.00**

Honoring God with the Tithe CD
Many people in the church today are not totally convinced that tithing is for today. They think that tithing is part of the law. Learn from the Word why tithing is for today and the blessings on tithers. If you don't tithe consistently, then you need to hear this! **$10.00**

The Power of Position CD -

When we settle in the wrong position – the wrong job, the wrong city, the wrong career, or the wrong ministry assignment – we hinder the blessings of God from flowing. Find out the four key steps to determining God's position for your life in this anointed teaching. **$10.00**

Kingdom Wealth CD -

God desires to prosper you financially. Some say that wealth is only mentioned in the Old Testament. This teaching will enlighten you to the New Testament teachings that show God desires for his people to manage large sums of money for His glory. **$10.00**

Order these valuable ministry resources online at:
www.VickySpringLove.org
www.ChangingYourMoneyMindset.com
or use the mail-in form on the next page.

After you implement the teachings,
please write us, we would love to hear
your testimonies of victory!

Dr. Vicky Spring Love would love to minister
at your church or conference, contact her at:

Dr. Vicky Spring Love
Victory Jubilee Publishing
P. O. Box 3286
Southfield, MI 48037-3286
248-354-3686
E-mail at: vickyspringlove@hotmail.com

Order Form

To order any of our ministry resources, please log onto the websites, or complete the information below. Please make checks or money orders payable to and mail to:

Victory Jubilee Publishing,
P. O. Box 3286, Southfield, MI 48037

ITEM (Please List)	**QUANTITY**	**TOTAL PRICE**
SUBTOTAL:		
SHIPPING $2.50 for 1 item **FREE SHIPPING on 2 or more items shipped to US.** $5.95 international shipping		
TOTAL:		

INFORMATION ON YOU:

Name______________________________________

Address____________________________________

City________________ State_______ Zip Code_________

Telephone (____)_______________

E-Mail Address:______________________________

Our Privacy Promise: We value your privacy and never sell or rent your personal information to any other company.

www.ingramcontent.com/pod-product-compliance
Lightning Source LLC
LaVergne TN
LVHW020627100826
845148LV00012B/2076
* 9 7 8 0 9 7 4 6 8 8 3 1 2 *